WAR ON THE MISSISSIPPI

Grant's Vicksburg Campaign

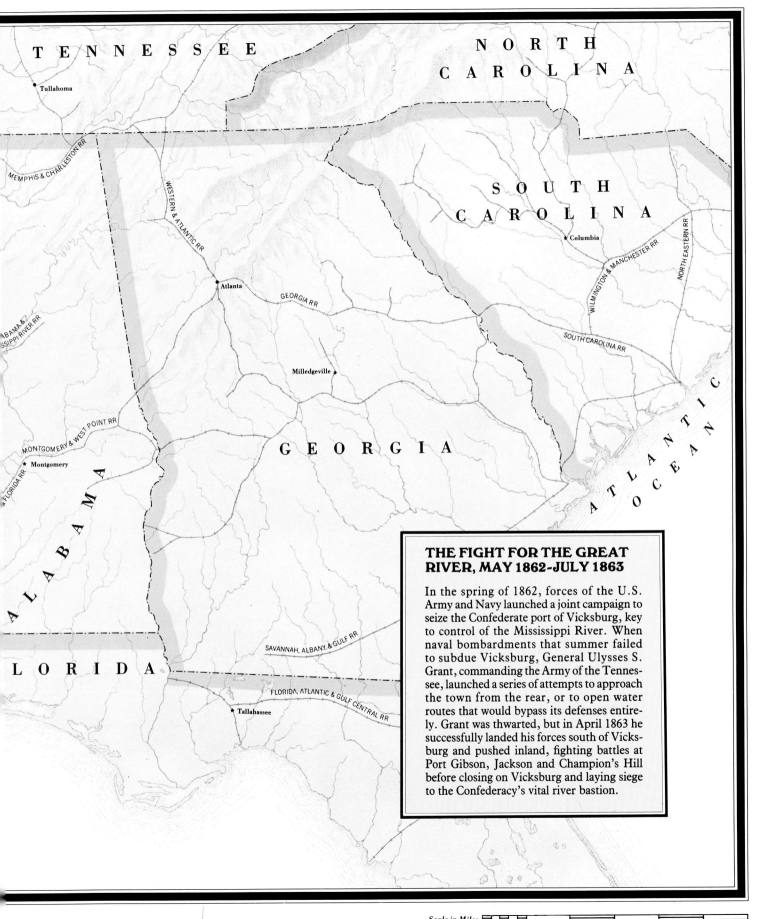

TENNESSEE

• Tullahoma

NORTH CAROLINA

SOUTH CAROLINA

• Columbia

MEMPHIS & CHARLESTON RR

WESTERN & ATLANTIC RR

• Atlanta

GEORGIA RR

ALABAMA & MISSISSIPPI RIVER RR

GEORGIA

Milledgeville ★

WILMINGTON & MANCHESTER RR

NORTH EASTERN RR

SOUTH CAROLINA RR

MONTGOMERY & WEST POINT RR

ATLANTIC OCEAN

FLORIDA RR

★ Montgomery

ALABAMA

SAVANNAH, ALBANY & GULF RR

FLORIDA

FLORIDA, ATLANTIC & GULF CENTRAL RR

★ Tallahassee

THE FIGHT FOR THE GREAT RIVER, MAY 1862-JULY 1863

In the spring of 1862, forces of the U.S. Army and Navy launched a joint campaign to seize the Confederate port of Vicksburg, key to control of the Mississippi River. When naval bombardments that summer failed to subdue Vicksburg, General Ulysses S. Grant, commanding the Army of the Tennessee, launched a series of attempts to approach the town from the rear, or to open water routes that would bypass its defenses entirely. Grant was thwarted, but in April 1863 he successfully landed his forces south of Vicksburg and pushed inland, fighting battles at Port Gibson, Jackson and Champion's Hill before closing on Vicksburg and laying siege to the Confederacy's vital river bastion.

Scale in Miles

0   25   50   100   150

TIME
LIFE
BOOKS

Other Publications:

HEALTHY HOME COOKING
UNDERSTANDING COMPUTERS
YOUR HOME
THE ENCHANTED WORLD
THE KODAK LIBRARY OF CREATIVE PHOTOGRAPHY
GREAT MEALS IN MINUTES
PLANET EARTH
COLLECTOR'S LIBRARY OF THE CIVIL WAR
THE EPIC OF FLIGHT
THE GOOD COOK
WORLD WAR II
HOME REPAIR AND IMPROVEMENT
THE OLD WEST

For information on and a full description of any of the
Time-Life Books series listed above, please write:
Reader Information, Time-Life Books
541 North Fairbanks Court, Chicago, Illinois 60611

This volume is one of a series that chronicles in full the
events of the American Civil War, 1861-1865.
Other books in the series include:

The Cover: A Federal flotilla under Rear Admiral
David Porter braves a storm of fire from Confederate
batteries along the shore and atop the high bluffs at
Vicksburg on the night of April 16, 1863. The transports and barges, lashed to the sides of Porter's
gunboats for protection, carry troops and supplies
downriver for Major General Ulysses S. Grant's
campaign to assault Vicksburg from the south.

THE CIVIL WAR

WAR ON THE MISSISSIPPI

BY

JERRY KORN

AND THE

EDITORS OF TIME-LIFE BOOKS

Grant's Vicksburg Campaign

TIME-LIFE BOOKS, ALEXANDRIA, VIRGINIA

The Civil War
Series Director: Henry Woodhead
Designer: Herbert H. Quarmby
Series Administrator: Philip Brandt George

Editorial Staff for *War on the Mississippi*
Associate Editors: Thomas A. Lewis (text);
Jane N. Coughran (pictures)
Staff Writers: Jan Leslie Cook, Glenn McNatt,
John Newton
Researchers: Kristin Baker, Brian C. Pohanka
(principals); Harris J. Andrews, Andrea E. Reynolds
Assistant Designer: Cynthia T. Richardson
Copy Coordinator: Stephen G. Hyslop
Picture Coordinator: Betty H. Weatherley
Editorial Assistant: Audrey Prior Keir
Special Contributors: Theodore V. Kruckel,
Paula York-Soderlund

Editorial Operations
Copy Chief: Diane Ullius
Editorial Operations: Caroline A. Boubin (manager)
Production: Celia Beattie
Quality Control: James J. Cox (director)
Library: Louise D. Forstall

Correspondents: Elisabeth Kraemer-Singh (Bonn);
Dorothy Bacon (London); Maria Vincenza Aloisi,
Josephine du Brusle (Paris); Ann Natanson (Rome).
Valuable assistance was also provided by Carolyn Chubet
(New York).

The Author:
Jerry Korn won the Distinguished Flying Cross as a B-24
copilot in World War II, and then worked as a reporter
for the Associated Press before becoming an editor for
Collier's and *Life.* He served for 12 years as the Managing Editor of Time-Life Books. He is also the author of
The Raising of the Queen, the story of a maritime salvage operation.

The Consultants:
Colonel John R. Elting, USA (Ret.), a former Associate
Professor at West Point, is the author of *Battles for Scandi-
navia* in the Time-Life Books World War II series and of
*The Battle of Bunker's Hill, The Battles of Saratoga, Mili-
tary History and Atlas of the Napoleonic Wars* and *American
Army Life.* Co-author of *A Dictionary of Soldier Talk,* he is
also editor of the three volumes of *Military Uniforms in
America, 1755-1867,* and associate editor of *The West Point
Atlas of American Wars.*

William A. Frassanito, a Civil War historian and lecturer
specializing in photograph analysis, is the author of two
award-winning studies, *Gettysburg: A Journey in Time* and
*Antietam: The Photographic Legacy of America's Bloodiest
Day,* and a companion volume, *Grant and Lee, The Virginia Campaigns.* He has also served as chief consultant to the
photographic history series *The Image of War.*

Les Jensen, Curator of the U.S. Army Transportation
Museum at Fort Eustis, Virginia, specializes in Civil War
artifacts and is a conservator of historic flags. He is a
contributor to *The Image of War* series, consultant for
numerous Civil War publications and museums, and a
member of the Company of Military Historians. He was
formerly Curator of the Museum of the Confederacy in
Richmond, Virginia.

Michael McAfee specializes in military uniforms and has
been Curator of Uniforms and History at the West Point
Museum since 1970. A fellow of the Company of Military
Historians, he coedited with Colonel Elting *Long Endure:
The Civil War Years,* and he collaborated with Frederick
Todd on *American Military Equipage.* He is the author of
Artillery of the American Revolution, 1775-1783, and has
written numerous articles for *Military Images Magazine.*

Library of Congress Cataloguing in Publication Data
Korn, Jerry.
  War on the Mississippi.
  (The Civil War)
  Bibliography: p.
  Includes index.
  1. Vicksburg (Miss.) — Siege, 1863.   2. Grant,
Ulysses S. (Ulysses Simpson), 1822-1885.
3. Mississippi — History — Civil War, 1861-1865 —
Campaigns.   I. Time-Life Books.
II. Title.   III. Series.
E475.27.K67 1985   973.7'34   84-16206
ISBN 0-8094-4744-4
ISBN 0-8094-4745-2 (lib. bdg.)

CONTENTS

1

Defiance from Vicksburg 16

2

The Bayou Experiments 56

3

A Beachhead on the East Bank 84

4

The Sweep to the Big Black 108

5

Closing the Ring 134

Vicksburg, Mississippi, was built on hills so steep that in places the streets had to be cobblestoned in order to give men and horses a foothold. In 1810 there was nothing on the site except a 17th Century Spanish ruin.

Imperiled City on the Bluffs

At the outbreak of war, Vicksburg, Mississippi, was a splendid place to live and to visit. A thriving trade by steamboat and railroad had transformed the frontier village into a bustling little city of wealth and cosmopolitan tastes. Situated atop a chain of hills overlooking a great horseshoe bend in the Mississippi River, Vicksburg was known to its proud residents as the "Queen City of the Bluff." In the words of a young local diarist, Lucy McRae, it was a place of "culture, education and luxury."

The city boasted its own orchestra, a theater with a repertory company that specialized in Shakespeare, three daily newspapers and a lecture hall. The citizenry was uncommonly literate. The British journalist William H. Russell, after attending a seminar on current affairs at the Vicksburg railroad station, reported that the participants were better informed on many issues than he was.

The booming commerce attracted a diverse population — a third of the 3,500 white residents were foreign-born — and spawned scores of enterprises, everything from genteel shops offering fine jewelry and the latest European fashions to rowdy saloons and gambling halls.

Vicksburg, shown here in a series of wartime photographs, was a rich strategic prize. But when fighting began in faraway South Carolina in 1861, the conflict seemed too distant to be harmful to Vicksburg. Deceptively, the War seemed no more threatening, a resident wrote, than the "low, rumbling thunder that one hears on a quiet summer day."

The Warren County Courthouse, completed in 1860 in the Greek Revival style on the city's highest point, was the pride of all Vicksburg. "A great many persons go up there in the evening," one citizen wrote to a relative. "The view from the top is very fine about sunset."

The three-story building owned by prominent merchant William Tillman so dominated the intersection at Clay and Washington Streets in Vicksburg's main business district that the area was called "Tillman's Corner."

Freight cars at Vicksburg's depot await a locomotive on the Southern Mississippi Railroad line, which linked Vicksburg with Jackson and Meridian to the east. Vicksburg's taxpayers partially subsidized the construction of railroads as a way of bringing more commerce to the city.

Steamboats crowd the wharves along Vicksburg's waterfront, a district notorious for its saloons, gambling halls and bawdy houses. When a prominent local doctor was shot and killed in one such establishment, a posse of vigilantes lynched five gamblers; other undesirables were tarred and feathered and set adrift on a raft in the Mississippi.

13

Fine residences of wealthy merchants and professional men dot the Vicksburg bluff in this photograph taken from the courthouse cupola looking north.

Defiance from Vicksburg

"Ships cannot crawl up hills 300 feet high, and it is that part of Vicksburg which must be taken by the Army."

COMMANDER DAVID DIXON PORTER, U.S. NAVY

In the summer of 1862 the attention of Americans both north and south was drawn to the town of Vicksburg, Mississippi, perched high on a bluff overlooking the great river. At that time, the bustling river port was the War's most strategic point. And in the desperate struggle to possess it, many soldiers would die.

Control of Vicksburg was essential to control of the Mississippi River. This had become increasingly evident as the Federal armies fought their way down the Mississippi from Cairo, Illinois, and up from the Gulf of Mexico. By early June 1862, with the capture of New Orleans and the neutralization of Fort Pillow, about 50 miles north of Memphis, the Union had a firm grip on the Mississippi at both extremes of the Confederacy. But the center remained in Confederate hands. And the focal point of Rebel resistance was Vicksburg.

Not only did the city command the central Mississippi, but it was also a critical transfer point for both rail and river traffic bound eastward toward the heart of the Confederacy. Moreover, one of the Confederacy's few rail links to the Southwest was the Vicksburg, Shreveport & Texas Railroad. The line had yet to live up to its name: In 1862 it ran only from Vicksburg to Monroe, Louisiana — less than halfway to Shreveport and the nearby Texas border. But still it was a vital conduit for supplies reaching Monroe by road and river. The eastern terminus was actually in the little village of De Soto, across

the river from Vicksburg. From there, a ferry carried freight across the Mississippi to be loaded on cars of the Southern Mississippi Railroad for the journey eastward. Most of the urgently needed beef and produce from Texas and Arkansas moved along this route. Perhaps as important, European arms, effectively denied to the South by the Union coastal blockade, found their way into the Confederacy via Mexico, Texas and that vital crossing at Vicksburg.

There was an alternate route for Texas farm goods headed east. Cargo vessels would steam down the Red River, a navigable waterway running across Louisiana from Texas and joining the Mississippi 200 miles south of Vicksburg. The boats would turn north upon reaching the Mississippi and unload their wares at the Vicksburg docks. The fall of New Orleans, although it was a severe blow to the Confederacy, had had little effect on this traffic.

In the view of Jefferson Davis, Vicksburg was "the nailhead that held the South's two halves together." Conversely, Vicksburg blocked Federal lines of communication on the Mississippi. The Midwest was already one of the nation's main agricultural areas, producing far more than Americans alone could use. Before the War, the region's surplus had been shipped down the Mississippi on barges, flatboats and cargo vessels, then transferred to oceangoing ships at New Orleans and carried to ports around the globe. But by the spring of 1862 the region had been

This sleeve patch, embroidered with an eagle perched on an anchor, identified U.S. Navy petty officers, including stewards and cooks, masters-at-arms, and boatswain's, gunner's and carpenter's mates.

choked off from the world for the better part of a year. So long as the South held Vicksburg, this avenue would remain blocked. Rail transport to Eastern ports was generally unavailable because of wartime priorities — and was prohibitively expensive in any case. The Midwest was suffering, and Washington was concerned that Westerners were losing their enthusiasm for the War.

The importance of Vicksburg was not lost on Abraham Lincoln. In his youth the President of the Union had traveled down the Mississippi on a flatboat, and he knew the river well. U.S. Navy Commander David Dixon Porter remembered Lincoln pointing to a map in early 1862 and remarking on the importance of the Confederate holdings in the West: "Here is the Red River, which will supply the Confederates with cattle and corn to feed their armies. There are the Arkansas and White Rivers, which can supply cattle and hogs by the thousand. From Vicksburg these supplies can be distributed by rail all over the Confederacy.

"Valuable as New Orleans will be to us," Lincoln continued, "Vicksburg will be even more so. We may take all the northern ports of the Confederacy, and they can still defy us from Vicksburg. It means hog and hominy without limit, fresh troops from all the states of the far South, and a cotton country where they can raise the staple without interference."

The Federal command laid plans to capture Vicksburg as early as possible. When Flag Officer David Glasgow Farragut left Washington in the spring of 1862 to mount his attack on New Orleans, he carried with him orders to capture Vicksburg as well.

It would not be an easy task, for Vicksburg possessed formidable natural defenses. The city proper stood on a series of frowning bluffs above the river. Fortifications along these precipices, which reached as high as 300 feet, protected the city from attack by river. The surrounding territory, including the countryside across the river in Louisiana, was a maze of bayous and bogs, much of it impassable to troops on foot. East of the city, the line of bluffs abruptly fell away to a plain; the hillsides commanded the eastern approaches. From almost any direction, Vicksburg was a nettle that could be grasped only with immense difficulty. Yet there had been a time when the river port could have been taken by any force that reached it. During the first year of the War, the city was guarded by only a token garrison, and the fortifications were incomplete.

The fall of New Orleans on April 26 galvanized the Confederate authorities — not to mention the people of Vicksburg, many of whom promptly fled their city. The next day a Vicksburg woman named Mahala Roach wrote in her diary: "This has been a singular Sunday, no Sabbath stillness has pervaded its air, but bustle and confusion have prevailed everywhere!" Merchants loaded their stock into wagons and clattered away; cotton was hauled out of warehouses to be burned before the Federals could get it; and families drove into the countryside in buggies and wagons. Meanwhile, other families, some from New Orleans, moved into Vicksburg, reasoning that they would be safer from the Federals in town. Unhappily, most of the people who moved out settled to the east of the city; a year later they would find themselves directly in the path of a Union army.

On May 1, grayclad troops began to arrive in Vicksburg; by the middle of the month there were about 3,500 of them, with more on the way. The first to appear were Louisianians up from New Orleans and its environs. Around Vicksburg, atop the bluffs, heavy guns were set up in batteries built by slave labor. By late May, 18 artillery pieces were in place. The city was not yet strongly defended, but at least it was no longer undefended. Farragut had missed a chance; if he had moved up the Mississippi right after the fall of New Orleans, Vicksburg might have been his.

Indeed, Farragut's orders had stipulated that he was to steam north immediately. The Federal plan called for him to run the Vicksburg batteries and link up with a squadron of gunboats making its way downriver from Cairo, Illinois, under Flag Officer Charles H. Davis. The two forces would then join in reducing the Vicksburg defenses. But most of Farragut's ships had been damaged during the battle for New Orleans, and Farragut took the time to repair and resupply them. Two weeks passed before Farragut started up the Mississippi.

Farragut was a good officer, intelligent and tough. At the age of 61, he was no longer young, but he was still fit. His tendency to testiness was redeemed by a sense of humor. On this campaign he would need it.

What Farragut required for the operation were river craft: flat-bottomed, shallow-draft side-wheelers and stern-wheelers. But the only vessels available were the seagoing wooden warships that he had brought to New Orleans. They were ill-suited for river warfare; their sails were of little use, their drafts too deep, their steam-powered screws vulnerable to damage in shallow water. Consequently, the fleet's progress upstream toward Vicksburg was a series of misadven-

tures. Ships frequently ran aground attempting to negotiate the narrow, twisting channels. There was not enough coal to fire the boilers, and the vessels had to stop frequently to take on wood. The roughly 1,400 soldiers, brought along to serve as a Vicksburg occupation force, huddled miserably aboard the transports, suffering from malaria and dysentery.

Still, some things went right. Baton Rouge, the Louisiana state capital, was defenseless and surrendered to the menace of the naval guns without firing a shot. At Natchez, Mississippi, a large crowd turned out in their Sunday best to view the fleet; the mayor, summoned to surrender the city, immediately did so. (Natchez was briefly reoccupied by the Confederates as soon as the Federal ships had passed, and the resident who had volunteered to carry Farragut's surrender demand to the mayor was jailed for treason; it took the intervention of General P.G.T. Beauregard to save him from execution.)

Most Natchez citizens seemed content to be neutral in the presence of the Federals, but one person revealed an allegiance. Commander David Dixon Porter, Farragut's foster brother, observed a young girl standing alone on the shore. Making sure no one was watching except Federal sailors, she whipped out a small U.S. flag, kissed it, and pressed it to her heart.

All of this seemed to bode well for Farragut's force as it approached Vicksburg: What had succeeded at Baton Rouge and Natchez should work there as well. But the Federals were in for a rude surprise. On May 18 an advance force aboard the sloop *Oneida* under Commander Samuel Phillips Lee slowly entered the bend of the river

Flag Officer David Glasgow Farragut fretted about the perils of sailing a deep-draft, oceangoing fleet on the shallow waters of the Mississippi, especially after his flagship *Hartford*, a 225-foot-long screw sloop, ran aground on the way to Vicksburg. "It is a sad thing," he commented, "to think of having your ship on a mud bank, 500 miles from the natural element of a sailor."

where Vicksburg stood, dropped anchor and sent a small boat shoreward under a white flag. When the boat was intercepted by a Confederate craft, the Federals handed over a message demanding the city's surrender.

Commander Lee and his men waited expectantly for five hours. Then the courier boat put out from the Vicksburg dock with the answer of the city authorities—an unequivocal no. The military governor of the city, Colonel James L. Autrey, declared: "Mississippians don't know, and refuse to learn, how to surrender." If the Federal commanders thought they could teach the Vicksburgers otherwise, he added, "let them come and try."

Farragut was taken aback by this unexpected response. He was not prepared for an assault on what now appeared to be a forbidding fortress. His ships' guns could not be elevated sufficiently to fire at the hilltop defenses; the Confederate batteries, on the other hand, were perfectly sited to bombard the ships below. An overland attack by the Federal infantry also seemed unfeasible. Brigadier General Thomas Williams, the officer commanding the contingent, pointed out the difficulties: The batteries would have to be silenced beforehand; he had but 1,400 men; and there were rumors that Rebel reinforcements numbering 20,000 men were on the way to Vicksburg.

Farragut could see no immediate solution to the problem. What is more, he had complained of feeling poorly in recent days. Had his health been better, he later suggested, he might have persisted in spite of the heavy odds. But under the circumstances, he decided to extricate himself. Calling the expedition a "reconnaissance in force," he returned to New Orleans, leaving only a few gunboats behind to observe the city.

But Farragut was not to get off so easily. The President and the Navy Department had expected great things from his upriver expedition, and they were astonished to learn that Farragut had not even attempted to run the Vicksburg batteries. The gunboats under Flag Officer Davis had begun their passage downriver from Cairo; a meeting between Farragut and Davis would at least mark the symbolic opening of the river. Assistant Secretary of the Navy Gustavus Fox sent an angry message to Farragut in New Orleans. Farragut must return to Vicksburg immediately. "The President," Fox said, "requires you to use your utmost exertions (without a moment's delay and before any other naval operations are permitted to interfere) to open the Mississippi and effect a junction with Flag Officer Davis." A peremptory order from the President could not be ignored, and on the 6th of June Farragut set out again.

As it happened, Davis too was still a long way from Vicksburg. On May 10 he and his flotilla had been attacked and severely mauled at Fort Pillow by a little fleet of Confederate rams — river steamers equipped with iron prows to hole enemy ships. The Confederates subsequently evacuated Fort Pillow on June 4, but the pesky force of rams still barred the route downriver from a new base at Memphis. Before Davis could rendezvous with Farragut, he would have to deal with those Confederate craft.

Davis was now much better equipped to cope with the enemy flotilla, however, for a fleet of Federal rams had joined him near Fort Pillow on May 25. Those vessels were the creation of Charles Ellet Jr., a brilliant 52-year-old civil engineer who had converted

nine steamboats to create Davis' ram fleet. Ellet, commissioned a colonel in the Federal Army, now captained the ram *Queen of the West*. His brother, Lieutenant Colonel Alfred W. Ellet, and his 19-year-old son, Charles Rivers Ellet, were also aboard ships in the ram fleet.

On June 6, as Ellet and his rams approached Memphis, the Confederate flotilla, under the joint command of Commodore James E. Montgomery and Brigadier General M. Jeff Thompson, came boldly out and launched an attack. But this time the Confederates were overmatched. The *General Lovell* was rammed by Colonel Ellet's *Queen of the West* and quickly went to the bottom. When two more Confederate rams, the *General Beauregard* and the *General Price*, converged to attack a Federal ram, they collided with each other instead. Both ran aground, and the *General Beauregard*, which had been riddled with Federal shells, was blown to pieces when her boilers burst. Four other Confederate vessels were put out of commission by volleys from Davis' gunboats. Three of these were badly damaged but salvageable.

Of the eight Confederate craft that had opened the fight, only one, the *General Van Dorn*, escaped downriver. More than 70 Confederates on the vessels were captured. The sole Federal casualty was Colonel Ellet; he suffered a bullet wound in the leg that later became infected and, on June 21, cost him his life.

The crowds of spectators watching the fight from the Memphis riverbank were staggered by the outcome. They had turned out in a holiday mood to cheer on their champions, only to see the fleet destroyed. Commodore Montgomery was killed aboard his flag-

An Artist's View of the River in Peacetime

In the late 1840s, St. Louis artist Henry Lewis and a team of assistants traveled extensively along the Mississippi River. Lewis was embarked on a grand venture: to create a huge panorama of the vast waterway.

After three years of labor, Lewis had painted a panorama that covered a strip of canvas 12 feet high and 1,300 feet long. With his mammoth work of art wrapped around a cylinder, he toured the United States, Canada and Europe, giving exhibitions. Lewis later repainted many of the best scenes in the popular romantic style of the period, and persuaded a German publisher to bring them out in a Mississippi Valley travelogue. These paintings, six of which are shown here, were universally praised. Wrote one American critic: "We recognize the locations as readily as if the reality was before us."

Henry Lewis and his men camp along the river. Their craft consists of two canoes topped by a cabin.

The steamboat *Grand Turk* takes on logs for its wood-burning boilers at a fueling station north of Baton Rouge, Louisiana.

A small schooner sits at anchor off the Mississippi River pilot station at the Southeast Pass leading into the Gulf of Mexico. No ship could safely negotiate the dangerous sandbars at the river's mouth without the guidance of an experienced pilot.

Crewmen of a flatboat maneuver their craft near the mouth of the Arkansas River, a major tributary of the Mississippi. In the background, a steamboat heads up the Arkansas toward Little Rock.

A polyglot fleet of riverboats lines the waterfront at Vicksburg, Mississippi, one of the South's most important transportation hubs.

An overseer carrying a whip supervises slaves harvesting cotton along the southern reaches of the Mississippi. "This view," wrote Lewis, "is one of hundreds of plantations on this part of the river."

ship, the *Little Rebel*. Meanwhile, General Thompson, commanding a small land force, was said to have stood by his horse on the bank and impassively watched the destruction of the flotilla; then, commenting, "They are gone and I am going," he had leaped onto his horse and galloped away.

Memphis was now unprotected. That afternoon, young Charles Rivers Ellet stepped ashore before a subdued citizenry and accepted the surrender of the city. Then Davis' squadron made its way downriver to a point a few miles upstream from Vicksburg to await David Farragut's ships.

The second time Farragut arrived at Vicksburg, on June 25, he was better prepared. He had more than twice as many troops aboard his transports — 3,200 in all — and accompanying the oceangoing vessels was a fleet of mortar schooners, which could easily lob their projectiles onto the heights. Farragut wasted no time. For two days, his mortars lay alongside the tree-lined bank and shelled the Vicksburg batteries. Then on the 28th Farragut left behind the slow-moving mortars and attempted to run the enemy batteries with his gunboats. The procession of 11 ships, moving slowly up the river in two columns, started in darkness at 2 a.m., and as the vessels drew alongside the city, they opened fire. To everyone's amazement, the broadside guns of the flagship *Hartford*, firing at maximum elevation, actually dropped some shells onto the shore batteries emplaced almost 200 feet above the river. But the other ships' guns, in the words of one captain, merely succeeded in firing "a perfect hailstorm against the slopes where no guns are." Meanwhile, the Vicksburg batteries (one of them commanded by Lincoln's brother-in-law, David Todd) poured a rain

of fire on the warships as they ran by.

Many of the Federal shells accidentally fell amid the homes of Vicksburg. A few shots dropped in the city during Farragut's passage in May, but this was the first heavy bombardment the residents had endured — the first of many to come — and its effect on the townspeople was numbing. "The roar of the cannon was continuous and deafening," wrote Confederate Brigadier General Martin Luther Smith. "Loud explosions shook the city to its foundations; shot and shell went hissing through the trees and walls, scattering fragments far and wide in their terrific flight; men, women and children rushed into the streets, and amid the crash of falling houses commenced their hasty flight to the country for safety." During this bombardment, Mrs. Alice Gamble became the first of Vicksburg's civilian war fatalities; she was struck by a shell fragment while trying to reach shelter.

Farragut's ships, meanwhile, blazed by Vicksburg's batteries. Only three of the 11 vessels had to turn back, and none suffered serious damage. However, one of Porter's mortar boats, the *Clifton*, was put out of action when a shot burst her boiler. Seven crewmen were scalded to death, and a sailor who jumped overboard drowned. In all, the Federals lost 15 dead and 30 wounded.

Farragut had achieved his objective, but the victory was hollow. He conceded that his run by Vicksburg had really served "no purpose." The Confederate defenses had been barely damaged; the powerful enemy batteries still commanded the river. Farragut wrote Secretary of the Navy Gideon Welles: "I am satisfied that it is not possible for us to take Vicksburg without an army force of twelve or fifteen thousand men."

The Federal troops on board Farragut's ships, 3,200 men led by Brigadier General Thomas Williams, were put ashore on the Louisiana bank. On the Mississippi side there were now 10,000 Confederate soldiers, and an assault on such a force was impossible. Instead, Williams had decided to try an experiment. Vicksburg was situated on a hairpin bend of the Mississippi. If a canal could be dug across the bend, the river might rush in and bypass Vicksburg entirely; in that case, of course, Union shipping could do the same. It seemed worth a try. Williams put his men to work with shovels.

The Confederates, meanwhile, were preparing a nasty surprise for Farragut. Some weeks before, a Confederate naval officer, Lieutenant Isaac Newton Brown, had been ordered to make a 180-mile voyage up the Yazoo River, which enters the Mississippi just north of Vicksburg. Brown's destination was the town of Greenwood. There the 45-year-old Kentuckian took possession of a partially completed vessel with a name — the *Arkansas* — but not much else attached to it. It was a hull and a collection of disassembled guns and engines. In the water nearby a scow had sunk with a load of railroad iron that had been intended to armor the boat's sides. From this unlikely assortment of materials Brown had been ordered to create an ironclad ram.

He set to work with a will. He moved the *Arkansas* downstream to Yazoo City, a more convenient location for the construction. The railway iron was retrieved from the water, floated down on a barge and bolted to a wooden frame atop the *Arkansas's* hull; to power his drills Brown used the hoisting engine of a steamboat tied up nearby. Carriages were constructed for the 10 smoothbores and

The Fighting Ellets and Their Fleet of Rams

Charles Ellet Jr. was a man obsessed. The 51-year-old engineer desperately wanted to serve the Union. For a year after war broke out he fired off to various Federal agencies one idea after another for defeating the Confederates. His favorite scheme involved a steam ram — a swift, metal-prowed vessel that could drive a hole in an enemy ship. Indeed, Ellet promoted this design so energetically that before long, in the words of one naval officer, he "had nearly gone insane on the ram question and had written and besieged the departments in Washington until they nearly went insane too."

Not until the spring of 1862 — after the Confederate ironclad ram *Merrimac* had wreaked havoc on Federal ships at Hampton Roads — did the government listen to Ellet. "He has more ingenuity, more personal courage, and more enterprise than anybody I have seen," admitted Secretary of War Edwin M. Stanton, who authorized Ellet to purchase and refit nine steamers as rams to use against Confederate ships in the Mississippi.

Ellet accomplished the task in 50 days. Given a colonel's commission, he was put in charge of the little fleet. As his second-in-command, he chose his brother Alfred; among his junior officers were his son Charles Rivers Ellet and his nephews Edward, Richard and John.

The fleet performed nobly at the Battle of Memphis; in less than an hour, an exuberant Ellet wrote to his daughter, the rams sank three enemy gunboats "absolutely and almost instantaneously," and damaged and captured two others. But the price of victory would prove fatally high. Ellet, who had been wounded in the leg, gradually weakened. Fifteen days after the battle, he was dead. His wife, Ellie, overcome by grief and exhaustion, followed him to the grave two weeks later.

COLONEL
CHARLES ELLET JR.

MEDICAL CADET
CHARLES RIVERS ELLET

LIEUTENANT COLONEL
ALFRED W. ELLET

LIEUTENANT COLONEL
JOHN R. ELLET

LIEUTENANT
EDWARD C. ELLET

LIEUTENANT
RICHARD ELLET

The Federal ironclad gunboat *Essex* takes on coal at Baton Rouge. The *Essex* was part of the river fleet that helped defend the Federal garrison occupying the town.

rifled guns; the engines were assembled and installed. Scarcely five weeks after he had started work, Isaac Brown had a wonderful homemade war machine — somewhat temperamental, particularly in the engine room, but swift, well protected and much more heavily armed than most rams.

Brown quickly recruited a crew — some of them artillerists and some from a Missouri infantry regiment — and on July 14 started down the Yazoo toward Vicksburg. There was little time to waste. The level of the river was going down, as it often did during the summer, and the *Arkansas,* drawing 13 feet, was in danger of being trapped. Moreover, Farragut's fleet was anchored in the Mississippi above Vicksburg, and Brown was not sure how much longer it would present such an inviting target.

On the trip downriver, the boiler of the *Arkansas* sprang a leak and soaked one of the powder magazines. Brown pulled in to shore

for a day to dry everything off in the sun — "expecting the enemy every moment," he wrote later.

The enemy was, in fact, on the way. Word of Brown's ambitious engineering project had reached Federal ears, and on July 15 three craft had been dispatched up the Yazoo to investigate. One of these vessels was the speedy ram *Queen of the West;* another was the light gunboat *Tyler,* and the third was the powerful ironclad gunboat *Carondelet,* captained by Henry Walke, a longtime friend of Brown's in the prewar Navy. The three Union boats were steaming up the river in line abreast when, suddenly, their astonished crews saw their quarry steaming toward them.

The Federal captains quickly realized that they were at a disadvantage. The *Queen of the West,* unarmed and unarmored, turned tail and headed back downstream, followed by the other two boats. They proved to be slower than the *Arkansas*, which opened fire as soon as it came into range.

The Federals fought back fiercely. In the spirited exchange, Brown suffered two head wounds; he said later that he knew he was all right when he brought his hand away from his injured skull and saw there were no brains showing. His pilot was mortally wounded. "Keep in the middle of the river," he told Brown as he was carried from the pilothouse. The Federals also suffered. The *Carondelet,* hit in her steering mechanism, ran aground. Brown fired one more volley at her and hurried off down the river.

But the *Arkansas* was now suddenly losing power. When the firing stopped—both the *Queen* and the *Tyler* had pulled ahead—

Brown had time to take stock. He found that the pipe connecting the furnace to the smokestack had been shot away, and flames were pouring into the boat's main cabin; the temperature there had reached 130°. Steam pressure had been reduced from 120 pounds to 20 pounds, barely enough power for steerageway. But the current was carrying her in the right direction, and Brown continued on his course, steaming out of the mouth of the Yazoo and into the Mississippi 10 miles north of Vicksburg.

The Federal fleet—"the greatest naval force hitherto assembled at one time in the New World," Brown later claimed—was lying at anchor three miles downstream, on both sides of the river. The Federals

The youthful crewmen of the 24-gun Union sloop *Hartford*, flagship of David Farragut, pose informally on deck. During engagements in the Vicksburg Campaign, Farragut stationed himself in the rigging and shouted orders to the crew through a speaking tube that ran from the mizzen top to the quarter-deck.

In an etching by a wartime artist, the Confederate ironclad ram *Arkansas* plows through the combined Federal fleets of Farragut and Flag Officer Charles Davis above Vicksburg on July 15, 1862. After the attack, the *Arkansas* took refuge under the Confederate batteries at Vicksburg. On shore, a Tennessee soldier watched the vessel arrive and later portrayed her (*inset*) in his primitive style.

had no steam up except for one vessel. They were caught by surprise when the *Arkansas* swept down on them.

Finding himself in a forest of masts and smokestacks, Brown let go with all his guns, firing rapidly, he recalled, "to every point of the circumference without fear of hitting a friend or missing an enemy." The *Arkansas* was moving too slowly to be used as a ram, but her guns were enough. Only once, Brown reported, did he take aim with his ship's prow, and then the boiler of the unidentified enemy vessel exploded before the Confederate could strike. "His steam went into the air," Brown recounted with satisfaction, "and his crew into the river."

The Union vessels could not maneuver, but they could fire their cannon. The air was full of shells. "The shock of the missiles striking our sides was literally continuous," Brown said. Most of the Federal projectiles ricocheted harmlessly off the sloping armor, or crossed the river and struck friendly vessels. But a few shots struck home with devastating effect, smashing the pilothouse, riddling the smokestack and penetrating the armor several times.

At length the *Arkansas* passed the fleet, and as she slowly limped into the welcome protection of the Vicksburg batteries, the cannonading died down. It had been a phenomenal exploit — one unknown Confederate officer and his jerry-built vessel tweaking the nose of a top Federal admiral and his whole fleet — and it had been witnessed with indescribable delight by a large audience of townspeople. Nevertheless, as the battered *Arkansas* drew into the Vicksburg docks the cheering died down. The ram's decks and deckhouse were a horrendous scene of carnage: Blood, hair, brains and bone fragments were everywhere. The *Arkansas* had suffered 12 killed and 18 wounded — and because she was a relatively small boat, the evidence of the human damage was widespread and chilling.

The Federals had fared much worse; they counted 17 dead and 42 wounded. The *Arkansas* had disabled one vessel and scored hits on many others; every wooden ship in Farragut's fleet had taken at least one hit.

Worst of all for the Federals was the humiliation they had suffered. David Farragut, sleeping late that morning, had tumbled from his bunk at the sound of gunfire and had watched the whole affair in his nightshirt. He was furious. His own flagship was one of the vessels damaged; his self-esteem had been damaged even more. "Damnable neglect, or worse!" he exclaimed after the shooting ended. He reported the episode to Secretary Welles "with deep mortification." Welles thought the mortification well-merited. The *Arkansas* attack, he wrote in his diary, was "the most disreputable naval affair of the war."

Farragut vowed vengeance, urged on by his superior in Washington. "It is an absolute necessity," Welles telegraphed, "that the neglect or apparent neglect of the squadron should be wiped out by the destruction of the *Arkansas*."

In fact, Farragut tried to even the score that very day. He ordered the fleet to sail immediately past Vicksburg. The vessels ran the batteries once more and this time blasted away at the Confederate ram as they went by at sunset. George Gist, one of Brown's officers, wrote: "The great ships with their towering spars came sweeping by, pouring out broadside after broadside, whilst the batteries from the hills, the mortars from above

and below and the ironclads kept the air alive with hurtling missiles and the darkness lighted up by burning fuses and bursting shells."

But the *Arkansas*, her sides colored dark red by rust from the iron rails protecting her, made a difficult target against the red clay of the bluffs and she suffered only minor damage. Farragut, however, lost five men killed and nine wounded; the gunboat *Winona* was disabled and had to be run ashore to keep her from sinking.

Farragut insisted on one more try, and several days later, on July 22, Flag Officer Davis sent two ships, the ironclad *Essex* and the ram *Queen of the West*, against the *Arkansas*. Commander Porter went on board the *Essex* to lead the attack. As the Federal ships opened fire, Brown executed a shrewd maneuver. He swung his vessel away from the bank, prow out, to present the smallest possible target. Consequently, neither Union vessel was at first able to land a solid blow.

Then, at great risk to his ship, Porter brought the *Essex* to within five feet of the *Arkansas* and poured fire into her side. Porter recalled: "We could distinctly hear the groans of her wounded." A shot passed through one of the *Arkansas's* gunports, and a large hole appeared in her armor. Porter was close enough to take the enemy ram by boarding, but the storm of fire from Confederate batteries and infantry on the bank dissuaded him. A shell fragment hit Porter in the head, cutting a slight gash. Finally the Federals gave up. The *Essex*, struck by 42 shots, somehow escaped major damage; the *Queen of the West* was riddled with balls, but she, too, remained intact and her crew suffered few casualties. The *Arkansas* lost seven killed and six wounded; but she had withstood another savage Federal attack.

Flames engulf the *Arkansas* four miles above Baton Rouge on August 6, 1862. Disabled by engine trouble, the vessel was set afire by crewmen to prevent her capture by the Federal gunboat *Essex (left)*.

In the last week of July, Farragut called it quits. He was worried about the steady lowering of the water in the river, and was pressed by another concern besides. The troops who were trying to dig the canal to bypass Vicksburg had been laid low by malaria and dysentery, and their commander, General Williams, was anxious to evacuate them to Baton Rouge for rest and medical aid. Farragut complied. The canal project was abandoned, the soldiers boarded the ships, and Farragut with great relief started back toward deep water. A few days later Davis led his squadron back upstream. The first attack on Vicksburg was over.

The *Arkansas* was ordered to proceed at full speed to Baton Rouge to assist in a Confederate effort to retake that city. She was almost at her destination when her overworked engines gave out, and she had to be beached. On August 5 the attack on Baton Rouge was repulsed, and the next day, with

enemy forces approaching, the Confederates destroyed the *Arkansas* to keep her from falling into Federal hands.

While all this activity was occurring on the river, Major General Ulysses S. Grant, who would play a key role in the effort to capture Vicksburg, was spending a fretful summer on the Tennessee-Mississippi border. Vicksburg was far from his mind.

In many ways the past year had been a good one for Grant. The man who had been working as a clerk for his father at the outbreak of the War was now commander of the great Army of the Tennessee, his name famous for his victories at Forts Henry and Donelson in February and at the bloody battleground of Shiloh in April.

But somehow since Shiloh everything had started to turn sour; in recent weeks he had endured a series of humiliations. His critics said that he had botched the Battle of Shiloh

GENERAL THOMAS WILLIAMS

and would have lost had it not been for the timely arrival of reinforcements. Stories circulated that Grant was a poor officer, and often a drunken one; his own soldiers were repeating these charges.

Grant's superior officer, Major General Henry W. Halleck, commander of all Federal forces in the Department of the West, had also disparaged Grant's performance at Shiloh. After the battle, Halleck, a prim man known in the prewar Army as "Old Brains," arrived on the scene and took direct control of the Army of the Tennessee, treating Grant with scant courtesy thereafter. Grant was not consulted about plans; he was not informed of military movements; he was given no important responsibilities. According to his friend, Major General William Tecumseh Sherman, Grant thought of resigning that summer, but Sherman talked him out of it.

When, in July, Halleck was ordered to Washington to become general in chief of the Federal Army, he summoned Grant to Corinth, Mississippi, not far from Shiloh. Halleck told Grant he was leaving, and added, "This place will be your headquarters." This seemed to augur increased responsibilities for Grant, but for two reasons he was less than delighted.

For one thing, despite the fact that Grant was the senior commander, Halleck was apparently looking for someone else to take charge of the military department in which Grant was operating. Halleck asked Secretary of War Edwin M. Stanton if the President had any suggestions, and then, when none were forthcoming, he offered the job to his chief quartermaster, Colonel Robert Allen. Allen declined it. How much Grant knew about this maneuvering is uncertain, but he could see the result. As a practical

matter, he later wrote wryly: "I became a department commander because no one was assigned to that position over me."

Grant's other reason for discontent was that Halleck's first act as general in chief was to cut Grant's department, reducing it to about half its former area and a half of its former troop strength. In the end, Grant had about 100,000 men under him—the Army of the Tennessee and Major General William S. Rosecrans' Army of the Mississippi. Major General Don Carlos Buell's 101,000-man Army of the Ohio, which had been under Grant at Shiloh, was sent to Kentucky and Tennessee to counter the threat to that area posed by Confederate forces under General Braxton Bragg.

Grant's shrunken command was spread across the southwestern corner of Tennessee. Sherman's division was protecting Memphis. One hundred miles to the east and just south of the Tennessee border, Major General Edward O. C. Ord's division was defending Corinth, Mississippi, now a major Union depot. General Rosecrans' army held the railroad from Corinth 20 miles east to Iuka. All Grant could do with his troops was defend his territory, which meant handing over the initiative to the Confederates—a galling circumstance for the combative general. He was sure the Rebels would attack someplace; there was nothing he could do now except wait.

There were two sizable Confederate forces in the region, one at Holly Springs, Mississippi, about 50 miles west of Corinth, and the other at Tupelo, about the same distance to the south. Early in September they both began to close in on Corinth. The force from Tupelo, led by Major General Sterling Price, headed northeast, and on Septem-

A Fight for Baton Rouge between Two Sick Armies

"They marched in straggling order, many of them lank, bent individuals, seemingly hardly able to support the burden of their blanket rolls and haversacks, but their rifles were clean and shining." Thus did a Confederate officer describe the 2,600-man force of General John C. Breckinridge that advanced on Baton Rouge, Louisiana, in August of 1862 to wrest the river port from its Federal occupiers. Earlier that summer, the same men had helped thwart the first Federal attempt to take Vicksburg. Now, many of them ill, some shoeless, others coatless and all of them weary and thirsty, they were on the offensive again.

Breckinridge, a former Vice President of the United States and one of Lincoln's opponents in the 1860 presidential race, planned to trap the Federal garrison between his troops, attacking from the east, and the Confederate ironclad ram *Arkansas*, which was steaming downriver to neutralize the Federal gunboats at Baton Rouge.

Alerted by rumors of the advance, Federal Brigadier General Thomas Williams (*left*) had ordered his men into battle positions. Although better supplied than the Confederates, Williams' troops were in little better condition; almost half the garrison of 4,000 was on the sick list.

The Confederates attacked early on the morning of August 5. Aided by a dense fog that shielded their movements, they drove back the enemy's left flank, taking a heavy toll among the Federal officers. Williams then galloped into the thick of the fighting. "Boys," he shouted, "your field officers are all gone. I will lead you." Moments later, the general fell, mortally wounded by a rifle ball in the chest.

But then the tide of battle turned. Unchallenged by the *Arkansas* — which had stalled upriver and would be destroyed by her crew the following day — the Union gunboats soon blunted the Confederate onslaught, and Williams' Federals succeeded in driving the Confederates back. By midmorning, the fighting was over. Baton Rouge remained in Federal hands.

When Breckinridge learned of the *Arkansas*'s fate, he was left with no choice but to withdraw. The Confederates had inflicted 383 casualties in the action for Baton Rouge; but they had suffered 456, including 84 dead — among them Lieutenant A. H. Todd, President Lincoln's brother-in-law. Their effort, however, was not entirely in vain. Fearing a second attack, the Federals retired two weeks later to the safer precincts of New Orleans.

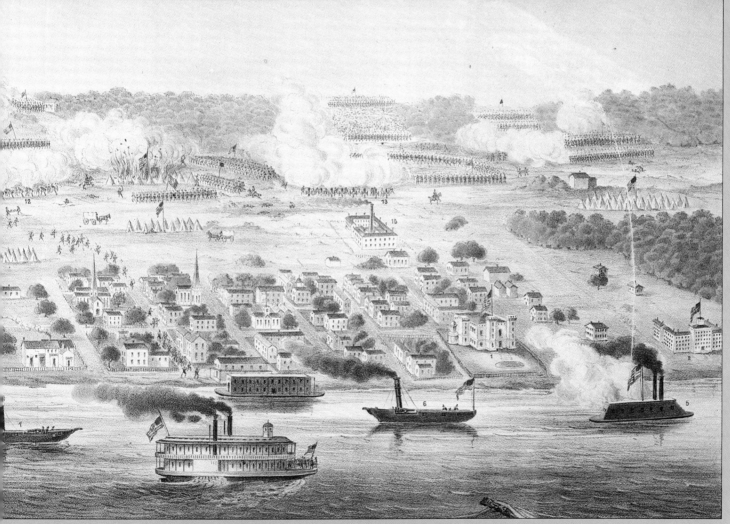

Federal troops, supported by an ironclad (*right*), clash with Confederates outside Baton Rouge. Some hard-pressed Federals on the left are retreating.

ber 14 seized Iuka, the pretty little resort town set in the rolling hills of northern Mississippi east of Corinth. Iuka was being used as a supply depot by the Federals, and Price's move — curiously unopposed by the Union commander, Colonel Robert C. Murphy of the 8th Wisconsin Regiment — brought the Confederates a trove of hardtack and salt pork.

Grant reacted swiftly. He ordered both Rosecrans and Ord to march on Iuka; if they could trap Price there they might destroy his force of 17,000 men before it could link up with the 10,000 Confederates advancing from Holly Springs under Major General Earl Van Dorn. Three roads led into Iuka; as Ord advanced along the one in the north, Rosecrans was to cover the two in the south. Grant joined Ord's men on the march.

The difficult tactical maneuver Grant was trying to execute — moving two separate forces against an enemy from opposite directions — required careful timing and good communications. Ord would arrive first. Grant commanded him to delay his attack from the north until he could hear the sound of Rosecrans attacking from the south. But, apparently because of some freak atmospheric condition, when Rosecrans' troops engaged the Confederates on September 19 neither Grant nor Ord heard a thing.

At 2:30 that afternoon, Rosecrans' vanguard ran into Price's cavalry pickets one and a half miles south of Iuka. The Confederate troopers galloped back to warn Price, who was at his headquarters in town. Just as Grant had hoped, Price was anticipating the arrival of Ord and had concentrated all of his infantry north of town.

But Price reacted so quickly and aggressively to this unexpected new threat from the south that it was the Federals who were sur-

prised. Straight away, he ordered Brigadier General Henry Little, his best divisional commander, to rush two brigades to the threatened point and accompanied Little to the front to see what they were up against.

Rosecrans' column was spread out over a great distance, and slow to deploy in line of battle. The wooded terrain particularly hampered the movement of the artillery. "Why in hell can't we let 'em have it?" asked an exasperated Federal gunner as he watched Little's Confederates swiftly assembling. "My God," cried another, "they're coming right here in the bush and are going to gobble the whole damned caboodle of us before we strike a lick!"

Little's men charged — straight at the 11th Ohio Battery. The Federal infantry brigade supporting the battery gave way, but the artillerymen stuck to their guns, firing canister point-blank at the onrushing Confederates. Before long, though, two Texas regiments overwhelmed the 80 Ohioans, killing 19 and wounding 35 — the greatest loss suffered by any artillery battery in the War.

While the fighting raged, Price and Little conferred on horseback near the front lines. Realizing that the Federals were in far greater strength than he had at first thought, Price ordered Little to send forward the rest of his division. No sooner were the words out of Price's mouth than a Minié ball struck Little flush in the forehead, killing him instantly.

In the confusion following Little's death, the Confederate attack let up long enough for the bulk of Rosecrans' troops to deploy. The reinforcements solidified his line, and the Federals recaptured the guns of the 11th Ohio Battery, only to be driven off again.

By the time darkness put an end to the seesaw fighting, the Federals had lost 825 men, including 141 killed. The Confederates suffered 693 casualties, with 86 dead.

Rosecrans was making plans to renew the fighting the next day when he discovered that Price had quietly slipped away. Rosecrans had unaccountably failed to guard one of the two southbound roads out of Iuka. The Federal forces did not follow the retreating Confederates, and a few days later, Price united his forces with Van Dorn.

During the next week or so it became apparent to the Federals that the real Confederate target was Corinth, and both sides built up their forces in anticipation of a new collision. Corinth, one of the principal rail junctions in the western Confederacy, was a valuable prize. Its loss after Shiloh had cost the Confederates one of their main East-West rail connections and had compelled them to give up Fort Pillow. Reclaiming Corinth would be a major achievement for the Confederacy — and it might weaken the Federal hold on the Mississippi.

Once again the principal Union field commander would be William Rosecrans, whose force now comprised two infantry divisions from his own Army of the Mississippi and two from the Army of the Tennessee, plus a small division of cavalry. Rosecrans was a complex man. He was a deeply religious Roman Catholic, whose profanity and the taking of God's name in vain were legendary throughout the Army — as was his almost ungovernable temper. And yet as a combat leader, he was beloved by his troops. "Old Rosy" visited his men often, saw that they were well fed and supplied, and — most important from their viewpoint — was always in evidence in battle, usually where the fighting was heaviest.

Corinth was defended by two sets of earthworks that guarded the northern approaches to town. One had been dug by the Confederates two or three miles outside the town. After the Federals captured Corinth, Grant ordered the second earthworks constructed on the edge of the town because he felt that the other line was too extended to defend adequately.

This time Rosecrans' adversary was to be Earl Van Dorn, a 42-year-old West Pointer who had been brevetted for gallantry in the Mexican War and had been regarded as one of the most dashing officers in the prewar Army. Born 20 miles south of Vicksburg near the town of Port Gibson, he had recently been placed in charge of the Vicksburg defenses. Van Dorn had scarcely assumed the post when he angered the residents of the city by imposing martial law. He had, in fact, never been popular there. He was known as a drinker and a womanizer (in May 1863 he would be shot to death by an outraged husband). Among strait-laced Southerners such

a reputation was anathema. But Van Dorn was bold to the point of rashness. Leading 22,000 troops, he approached Corinth from the northwest, advancing along the Memphis & Charleston Railroad. He would strike from that direction for what seemed an excellent reason. Some weeks before, a young woman from Corinth — only her last name, Burton, was recorded — had sent him a note describing the entrenchments around the town and pointing out that they were weak on the northwest side. The note had been intercepted by the commander at Corinth, General Ord, who read it, resealed it and after a time sent it on to its destination. The defenses had in fact been weak at the time the note was written, but had since been strengthened by the addition ordered by Grant. Instead of attacking one line of earthworks, as Van Dorn expected, the Confederates would face two.

On the other hand, Rosecrans' Federal force was equal to Van Dorn's only in size. Many of the Federal regiments were poorly trained; the morale of the men was low and dysentery was rampant in the ranks.

Early on the morning of October 3, 1862, Van Dorn launched his three divisions in a headlong attack on the outlying Federal entrenchments. The heaviest assault fell on Brigadier General Thomas A. Davies' division in the center of the Federal line. Davies reported that his artillery "mowed lanes through the solid columns" of Confederates, but still they came on. Soon Van Dorn's men had split the Federal line and driven it back. All three of Davies' brigade commanders were wounded as they struggled to rally their men — one of them, Brigadier General Pleasant A. Hackleman, would die of his injuries. A disorganized mob of soldiers fell back to-

ward Corinth, but when they came to the troops manning the recently constructed earthworks on the outskirts of town, they regrouped and stood their ground.

For the rest of the day fighting raged around the earthworks, but neither side could gain the upper hand, and darkness put an end to the fighting. Van Dorn and Rosecrans each insisted afterward that with one more hour of daylight he would have won the battle that day.

At 10 a.m. the next day, October 4, Van Dorn resumed the offensive in 90° heat; General Rosecrans noted that the Confederates "advanced splendidly." Their strongest effort was against the Federal center; there Confederate Brigadier General John C. Moore led five regiments against an earthwork known as Battery Robinett. One of those defending the battery, 22-year-old Captain Oscar Jackson of the 63rd Ohio, later recalled the attack: "They formed one column of perhaps 2,000 men in plain view, then another. I thought they would never stop coming out of the timber. As soon as they were ready they started at us with a firm, slow, steady step. In my campaigning I had never seen anything so hard to stand as that slow, steady tramp. Not a sound was heard, but they looked as if they intended to walk right over us." Brigadier General David S. Stanley, whose division now held the Federal center, wrote, "Should God spare me to see many battles, I never expect to see a more grand sight."

As the Confederates advanced, Captain Jackson kept an apprehensive eye on his Ohio men. They were staring at the spectacle of the approaching gray battle lines, fidgeting as they waited — shifting their feet, "pulling at their blouses, feeling if their cartridge boxes or cap-pouches were all right."

As General Moore's men neared Battery Robinett, the Federal artillery opened up with what one officer called a "storm of iron." To another defender it looked as if the shrapnel and shells were "mowing the surface of the ground." But still Moore's regiments came on, increasing their pace. Then the Federal infantry opened fire.

Among the Confederates on the receiving end was Lieutenant Charles Labuzan of the 42nd Alabama. "We were met by a perfect storm of grape, canister, cannon balls and minie balls," he wrote. "Oh God! I have never seen the like! The men fell like grass."

Even so, Moore's troops lost little momentum. They plowed into two Federal regiments aligned in front of Battery Robinett. Nine of 13 officers in the 63rd Ohio went down, including the regiment's colonel, who was shot from his horse. The Federals fell back. The Confederates scrambled over and through a tangled abatis before Battery Robinett, then surged on toward the earthwork. Lieutenant Labuzan recalled, "I saw men, running at full speed, stop suddenly and fall upon their faces, with their brains scattered all around. Others, with legs and arms cut off, shrieking with agony. The ground was literally strewn with mangled corpses. Ahead was one continuous blaze."

Facing the onslaught, a Federal soldier behind the battery watched in awe. "As they approached the works they were met by a withering fire," he recalled, "but they swept right on over the battery. Oh! It was a sublime thing to see."

Colonel William P. Rogers of the 2nd Texas was in the vanguard of the Confederate attack, carrying his regimental flag. "He looked neither right nor left, neither at his own men nor at mine," a Federal officer said, "but with eyes partly closed, like one in a hail storm, was marching slowly and steadily upon us."

But without warning, the swarming Confederates received a severe blow. As they scrambled up the parapet and crested the earthwork, the 11th Missouri and 27th Ohio regiments, which had been lying prone 30 yards behind Battery Robinett, rose up and fired a terrible volley into the attackers. Colonel Rogers fell, riddled with bullets; Lieutenant Labuzan watched as men "rolled down the embankment in ghastly heaps."

Private J. A. McKinstry and 15 of his comrades from the 42nd Alabama were on the wall of the works when the deadly volley came. "A minie ball went crashing through my left hip and turned me half around," McKinstry recalled. "Another went tearing through my right shoulder, which changed my position to front; and another ball crushed through my left shoulder, causing me to drop my gun and my left arm to fall limp by my side. I looked, and everyone of the fifteen who were standing with me had fallen in a heap." Cradling his useless left arm in his right, McKinstry scrambled back down the wall of the fort and, despite his hip wound, "ran for half a mile before I fell."

By now three of General Moore's five regimental commanders had fallen, but still the Confederates pressed on. The flag of one Arkansas regiment was torn to pieces by Federal bullets, but the color-bearer kept moving. He was last seen alive, Moore reported, "going over the breastworks, waving a piece and shouting for the Southern Confederacy." Yet for all the bravery, the assault was doomed. Fresh Federal troops charged into the fray, and after a brief hand-to-hand

Federal Major General William S.
Rosecrans was in high spirits after the
first day of fighting at Corinth, which
left the Confederates outside the
earthworks bordering the town. He
exulted to his commanders: "We've
got them where we want them."

struggle on the wall of the fort, the surviving Confederates broke for the rear. "I could see men falling as they attempted to run," Labuzan recalled, "some with their heads torn to pieces and some with the blood streaming from their backs. It was horrible. Our boys were shot down like hogs and fell back each man for himself."

As the attack receded and the smoke of battle dissipated, the defenders of Battery Robinett were presented with a gruesome sight. As one Federal wrote, "The ground was covered so thickly with gray coated men that one could scarcely step without stepping on them. The ditch was literally full and the parapet covered as thick as they could lie — in some places two or three deep."

Van Dorn's attack against the Federal right flank was slightly more successful. Exhibiting what one Northern officer called "a desperation seldom paralleled," Colonel W. H. Moore's brigade pierced the Federal line, captured a redoubt and overran a battery. Soldiers of the 20th Arkansas fought their way into the streets of Corinth itself. But there they were cut off and their colonel killed. Rosecrans regained the lost ground, and by 11:30 a.m. the fighting was over. Van Dorn's attack had failed disastrously, and his army was in full retreat to the northwest, back up the railroad line.

As Rosecrans walked over the battlefield, his gloves stained with the blood of a wounded aide, he saw an injured Arkansas lieu-

On the second day of the battle, Colonel William P. Rogers of the 2nd Texas, still holding his regimental colors, falls dead in the arms of a comrade after gaining the parapet of Battery Robinett. At right, the 27th Ohio and 11th Missouri begin the bayonet charge that would force the Confederates to retreat.

tenant leaning against a tree. "It's pretty hot fighting here," Rosecrans said. "Yes, General," replied the man, "you licked us good — but we gave you the best we had in the ranch."

Rosecrans had been given strict orders by Grant to keep the pressure on the Confederates if they were driven back. But Rosecrans' men were worn out, and he always thought of his men. "I directed them," he said, "to proceed to their camps, provide five days' rations, take some needed rest, and be ready early next morning for the pursuit." When Grant learned of the delay, he was disgusted. He later commented dryly: "Two or three hours of pursuit on the day of the battle, without anything except what the men car-

ried on their persons, would have been worth more than any pursuit commenced the next day could have possibly been."

As it happened, when Rosecrans started after Van Dorn the next day he accidentally took the wrong road and never did catch up with the retreating Confederates. Another Federal force, thoughtfully placed by Grant at a bridge on the Confederates' line of retreat, did some damage, but most of Van Dorn's battered Confederates simply moved to another bridge and continued on their weary way.

Once again, it had been a small fight, as such affairs were measured in the Civil War, but it had been a ferocious one. The Federal forces, fighting largely from behind breastworks, had suffered 2,839 casualties. The Confederates had suffered almost double that number — 4,838 killed, wounded or captured, more than 20 per cent of their total complement.

On the 30th of October, Rosecrans was transferred to Nashville, Tennessee, succeeding General Buell in command of the newly created Army of the Cumberland. Grant professed himself to be "delighted": Rosecrans, he felt, was not good at coordinating with fellow officers and would do better with an independent command. Rosecrans' future under Grant would have been highly problematical; according to one account, Grant "had intended to relieve him from duty that very day."

One month after the battle at Corinth, Van Dorn was brought before a court of inquiry to face charges brought by one of his most capable subordinates, Brigadier General John S. Bowen. The accusations included incompetence, drunkenness and "cruel and improper treatment" of his troops. Van Dorn was fully acquitted but was soon afterward removed from his post as commander of Vicksburg's defenses and placed in charge of Confederate cavalry in northern Mississippi, a job for which he was better suited by virtue of his prior cavalry service and his reckless zeal in combat.

On October 25, 1862, Ulysses S. Grant was formally named commander of the Department of the Tennessee, which now included everything along the Mississippi River south of Cairo. Grant sent a proposal to Halleck in Washington. He wanted to stop protecting railroads and supply depots and begin to move south toward an objective worthy of some effort: Vicksburg.

Federal soldiers survey the carnage in front of Battery Robinett on the day after the Battle of Corinth. The body of Colonel William P. Rogers, who led the Confederate assault, lies just left of the tree stump at center, near his dead horse.

Garrison Duty at a Whistle Stop

To General Ulysses S. Grant, the town of Corinth, Mississippi, situated at the junction of two major railroads, was "the great strategic position of the West between the Tennessee and the Mississippi Rivers." But to the tens of thousands of Federal soldiers garrisoned at Corinth, the place was nothing but a dry, dusty Southern crossroads.

The first troops arrived in late May of 1862 to find Corinth's water supply — barely adequate for the 1,000 townspeople alone — dwindling fast and badly

The Tishomingo Hotel, next to Corinth's rail depot, served as a hospital during the Union occupation. It was renowned then for dispensing a singular luxury: ice wate

contaminated by the more than 50,000 Confederate soldiers who had just departed the area. Soon, a drought turned the wells and stream beds bone dry.

"We have to go a mile and a half for water and after we get it, it's not fit to drink," one soldier grumbled. A Northern reporter wrote: "With every pint of fluid, one has to drink a half ounce of dirt. After it gets to the stomach, it lays as heavy and indigestible as a bed of mortar." Diarrhea and dysentery spread throughout the ranks, laying low about a third of the men. Even the generals suffered: At one point, Henry Halleck, John Pope and William T. Sherman were all prostrated by what the soldiers dubbed "the Mississippi quick-step."

Flies and mosquitoes added to the misery, along with a pest unfamiliar to the Northerners: As one Wisconsin man recalled ruefully, "Here for the first time, was encountered upon his native heath, the chigger. His mission was to eat and die. Every soldier was a walking chigger cemetery."

With the exception of the battle in October 1862, the duty was dull, enlivened only by occasional expeditions into the countryside after Confederate guerrillas. To keep busy, many of the soldiers took up their peacetime trades, working for the camp as blacksmiths, gunsmiths, photographers and carpenters.

Finally, the Federal advance deeper into the South rendered the occupation of Corinth unnecessary, and in January 1864 the Federals pulled out, leaving the residents to reclaim their town.

Soldiers of the 52nd Illinois stand at rest in front of their barracks. On the hill behind them are Federal earthworks, where bloody fighting took place in October 1862

Their belongings packed in a wagon, former slaves wait to see Corinth's provost marshal, the Federal administrator of the occupation. Blacks from the surroundin

...untryside journeyed to Corinth to work as laborers and domestic servants in exchange for food, tobacco and clothing.

Federal troops guard cotton bales near the Corinth Hotel. Despite the risk of reprisal from Confederate guerrillas, some local farmers sold cotton to the Northerner

Their arms stacked, men of the 52nd Illinois gather outside barracks they built out of lumber stripped from deserted buildings in Corinth.

The Bayou Experiments

By early November 1862, General Grant had set in motion a plan for the speedy conquest of Vicksburg. Gathering forces as he went, he began moving slowly southward from the Tennessee border along the tracks of the Mississippi Central Railroad. His course was parallel to the great river and about 60 miles to the east. He planned to sweep inexorably through Mississippi, carefully extending and maintaining his lines of supply as he progressed, until he reached Jackson. There he would cut the railroad line between that city and Vicksburg, and flank the river port — at which point he expected to take Vicksburg with relative ease, if it did not first surrender.

Strangely enough, Grant was not the only general contemplating an attack on Vicksburg. Even as Grant commenced the campaign, he was hearing persistent rumors that another Federal commander — Major General John McClernand — was raising an army north of the Ohio River and that he intended, with Washington's blessing, to move down the Mississippi and launch an amphibious attack on the port.

Grant could scarcely believe that such an operation would be mounted in his department without consultation. Yet troops recruited by this rival general soon arrived on the scene.

Grant was bewildered, and with good reason. He was witnessing the result of several months of behind-the-scenes political maneuvering that would affect the Vicks-

burg Campaign as much as anything the Confederates did.

Before the War, John McClernand had been a Democratic Congressman from Illinois. A staunch supporter of the war effort, he had been appointed a general in 1861 and had served in most of the Western campaigns under Grant. He was regarded as a reasonably competent officer, but certainly not one of the best. His ambition, however, knew no bounds. He was a notorious self-promoter, given to issuing boastful messages to his troops after every engagement.

Late in the summer of 1862, McClernand had approached Lincoln with a plan to lead a new levy of Illinois troops down the river to take Vicksburg. After Shiloh, the Federal advance in the West had stalled. McClernand knew the pressure Lincoln was under from Western farmers to open up the Mississippi, and he proposed to solve that problem, hoping in the process to earn new glory and advancement for himself. Lincoln — well aware of McClernand's home-state popularity, not yet sure of Grant's ability, and weary of slow-moving commanders such as George McClellan and Don Carlos Buell — approved the proposal over General in Chief Halleck's opposition.

McClernand was enormously encouraged when his direct appeal to the President succeeded. Unquestionably, he had won a political victory. But he had also won the quiet enmity of Halleck and Secretary of War Stanton — the officials he had bypassed in

This powder flask, made in the 1840s and embossed with an anchor design, was of a type issued with some naval rifles and muskets for use on Federal ships, including vessels on the Mississippi.

going to the President — and they began to cut McClernand down to size. Thus the official orders issued to McClernand gave him substantially less independence than he had envisioned; he was to lead the new Illinois regiments against Vicksburg, but there were two crucial qualifications. He could make his move, read the orders, only "when a sufficient force not required by the operations of General Grant's command shall be raised." Moreover, McClernand's operation was "subject to the designation of the general-in-chief." In other words, Grant would remain in overall command, and Halleck intended to keep a tight rein on the operation.

When Grant got wind of McClernand's politicking, he shot off a message to Halleck, demanding to know what was going on. "Am I to understand," he telegraphed on November 10, "that I lie still here while an expedition is fitted out from Memphis, or do you want me to push as far south as possible? Am I to have Sherman under my orders, or is he reserved for some special service?" The answer was swift and seemed decisive: "You have command of all troops sent to your department, and have permission to fight the enemy where you please."

But the question of McClernand was deliberately left unresolved. Puzzling over the matter, Grant continued to execute his plan for a land attack on Vicksburg, reaching the town of Oxford, 40 miles below the Tennessee border, early in December. By that time, however, he had concluded that the authorities in Washington were tolerating McClernand's activities because they wanted an amphibious campaign by way of the Mississippi River; if so, Grant was determined to lead it, and he began to revise his entire strategy.

Grant intended to foreclose McClernand's ambitions by launching an attack on Vicksburg from the river while McClernand was still in Illinois. Grant would divide his recently assembled army and launch a two-pronged movement southward. Major General Sherman would command an expedition of 30,000 men to be transported by Admiral David Porter's fleet down the Mississippi to the mouth of the Yazoo, just north of Vicksburg. There the troops would debark for an assault at a place called Chickasaw Bluffs. It was formidable terrain for an attack, but Sherman hoped to surprise the Confederates. To ease Sherman's task, Grant would continue his southward movement parallel to the Mississippi and try to distract the Vicksburg defenders.

Grant instructed Sherman to get started immediately. As he would later explain candidly: "I feared that delay might bring McClernand."

As often happened to commanders in the field, Grant frequently was distracted from his military and political problems by administrative ones. Two in particular were giving him trouble in late 1862, and both would have unexpected consequences.

Escaped slaves — now freedmen under the Emancipation Proclamation — had gathered in great numbers around Federal military encampments, Grant's included. Orders from Washington afforded these blacks the protection of the Army. But protection was one thing, subsistence another. "Humanity," Grant said, "forbade allowing them to starve." But thousands were crowding about his main camp — so many that it was virtually impossible to feed and shelter them. What is more, the destitute hordes were an actual impediment to the army's movement. Something had to be done.

Grant called in Chaplain John Eaton of the 27th Ohio Infantry and put him in charge of the freedmen. Eaton was an energetic young man in his early thirties who had served as superintendent of schools in Toledo before attending theological seminary. He attacked the problem with a will. Following a general outline laid down by Grant, Eaton established camps for the former slaves, provided medical treatment for those who needed it and found paid work for the able-bodied on local plantations where corn and cotton were going unpicked. In addition, he arranged for freedmen to pick the cotton growing in the numerous abandoned fields in the area. The bales were then shipped north and sold by the government, with a share of the proceeds going to the black laborers. "All at once," Grant reported with satisfaction, "the freedmen became self-sustaining." Later, after the War, Grant's approach was adopted by the federal government in setting up the Freedmen's Bureaus to deal with the problems of the millions of former slaves.

Grant's system might not have succeeded so well had wartime cotton been less valuable. As it was, cotton had become so precious that it was the source of another problem. Direct cotton trade between Federal and Confederate states was, of course, banned. But the prohibition had created great financial pressure; Northern industries deprived of the South's cotton needed it badly, while Southern growers with cotton piling up on their plantations desperately sought a way to sell it. The inevitable consequence was a large and enormously profitable black market.

A certain amount of surreptitious cotton traffic was winked at by officials on both sides. But Federal field commanders were being driven to distraction by Northern speculators who boldly followed their armies around, picking up cotton cheap and selling it for high prices in the North. Some of these traders were actually in the Army.

One day Grant received an unexpected visit from his father, Jesse Grant, who had brought along some friends from Cincinnati by the name of Mack. Grant welcomed them — until he discovered that the Macks were cotton speculators hoping to use his father as a way of getting at the supplies in the general's jurisdiction.

Grant was furious. He sent the Macks packing; he then drew up and circulated an order that was meant to put an end, once and for all, to cotton speculation. The wording of the order, however, was ill-advised and offensive in the extreme. The Macks, like many other traders, were Jewish, and the order focused on this fact. Its first sentence read: "The Jews, as a class violating every regulation of trade established by the Treasury Department and also department orders, are hereby expelled from the department within twenty-four hours from receipt of this order."

There was a howl of outrage. Jewish publications attacked Grant; rabbis preached against the order; Jewish organizations protested to members of Congress. The most effective action was taken by a man named Cesar Kaskel, a strong pro-Unionist who lived in Paducah, Kentucky, where 30 Jewish families had been forced to leave their homes because of Grant's order. Kaskel took a train to Washington, enlisted the help of a sympathetic Congressman, and went with

him to visit Abraham Lincoln. Lincoln listened with growing concern to Kaskel's complaint and then, in his presence, wrote a note to Halleck instructing him to see that the order was canceled forthwith. Halleck commanded Grant to rescind his order, and Grant immediately did so.

According to his wife, Grant later confessed that Congressional criticism of what she called "that obnoxious order" was well deserved. "He had no right," as she put it, "to make an order against any special sect." The general had stirred up a hornet's nest, and he was vastly relieved when the fuss finally died down and he could turn his full attention to Vicksburg.

The Confederates, in the meantime, had been making extraordinary efforts to improve their defenses in the Vicksburg area. Jefferson Davis, whose own Brierfield plantation was just a short distance down the Mississippi from Vicksburg, considered the town to be nothing less than "the vital point" of the Confederacy. He had sent Lieutenant General John C. Pemberton, a man he much admired, to take charge of Confederate forces in Mississippi, and then had installed over him as commander in the West one of the South's great officers, General Joseph E. Johnston.

Davis and Johnston visited Vicksburg on December 19 — shortly after Sherman began his move downriver — and two days later they traveled by train to Grenada, 60 miles south of Oxford. Pemberton and his army were there, keeping watch on Grant.

Johnston said later that serious differences emerged immediately among the three men at Grenada: Pemberton and Davis believed that the Confederates should defend

Vicksburg by turning it into a fortress, while Johnston advocated smashing the Federal forces wherever they could be found. This conflict was never resolved, and it would have disastrous consequences for the Confederate cause.

Davis and Johnston soon departed, and Pemberton was left in charge. The 48-year-old Pemberton was a West Point graduate and an able soldier, but he tended to be inflexible and convention-bound. Nevertheless, prior to the visit with Johnston and Davis, he had conceived and set in motion a bold plan — a double-barreled raid on the Federal rear. Grant, to feed his army as it moved toward Grenada, had set up a supply base at the northern Mississippi town of Holly Springs; it was the terminus of a long and difficult supply route from Columbus, Kentucky, almost 200 miles away.

Pemberton ordered Major General Van Dorn, now in charge of his cavalry, to descend on Holly Springs and cut Grant's supply line. Meanwhile, in a second offensive thrust, Brigadier General Nathan Bedford Forrest, an unorthodox but highly effective cavalry officer, was dispatched from below Nashville by General Braxton Bragg, commanding the Confederate Army of Tennessee. Forrest's mission was to strike the supply line around Jackson, Tennessee.

Grant had perceived the danger, and had sent warnings to his officers, including the commander at Holly Springs — Colonel Robert Murphy of the 8th Wisconsin, who had proved so ineffectual at Iuka three months earlier. Despite the alert, Murphy was caught unprepared when Van Dorn struck at daylight on December 20. Most of the Federal garrison of 1,500 men surrendered without firing a shot. Only one unit

Former slaves of Joseph Davis, brother of the Confederate President, assemble for a photograph with a Federal soldier on Davis' plantation near Vicksburg. The U.S. Army hired freed slaves for such tasks as digging trenches and working abandoned plantations.

chose to fight — Major John J. Mudd's 2nd Illinois Cavalry. With flashing sabers, his 350 troopers charged through the attacking Confederate cavalrymen, losing 100 men but making good their escape. Otherwise, the Confederates had the day to themselves, destroying a huge stock of supplies — $400,000 worth by Grant's estimate, $1.5 million worth by Van Dorn's. Shortly afterward, Murphy was cashiered from the Army for "cowardly and disgraceful conduct."

While Van Dorn was wrecking Holly Springs, Forrest was leading his Tennessee cavalry brigade against the Federals near Jackson, Tennessee. He was forced to fight hard, and in a series of engagements lost nearly 200 men, but by the time he pulled his troopers out, Grant's line of communications had been cut at a second point.

Indirectly, the Forrest raid was disastrous to General McClernand's inflamed ambitions. For almost three weeks, McClernand had been informing Washington from Illinois that his recruiting work was done and that he was now prepared to move on Vicksburg. However, the all-important orders permitting him to do so did not arrive. At length McClernand sent a distraught message to President Lincoln and Secretary Stanton: "I believe I am superceded. Please advise me."

Stanton replied blandly that Grant was organizing McClernand's recruits, and that orders designating McClernand as commander of Grant's XIII Corps were on their way. This was hardly the starring role McClernand had envisioned for himself. He was disturbed to find himself still under Grant's command, and he soon became furious when even those orders failed to come through. This delay was not Grant's fault;

General John C. Pemberton, commander of the Confederate defenses in Mississippi, was suspected of divided loyalties because he was a native of Pennsylvania. Actually, through years of prewar duty in the South and the influence of his Virginia-born wife, Patty (*above*), Pemberton had acquired a lasting devotion to the region.

as soon as he was instructed to do so by Washington, he had issued orders placing McClernand in command over Sherman. But Forrest had cut the telegraph lines. The orders went nowhere, and while Sherman approached Vicksburg, McClernand fumed in Springfield.

The two Confederate raids had a far more serious effect on Grant's situation. He was now caught in enemy territory without supplies, and he had to hustle back to Memphis the way he had come. He sent word to Sherman shortly before Christmas that his part of their two-pronged attack was no longer possible. But with communications in disarray, Grant's message arrived too late to stop the waterborne attack.

Sherman and Porter were still hoping to fall without warning upon the Vicksburg defenses. "The essence of the whole plan," Sherman wrote, was "to reach Vicksburg as it were by surprise." But the attempt at secrecy was doomed. Neither Grant nor Sherman knew that before the War a planter had installed a private telegraph wire along the west bank of the Mississippi north of Vicksburg. The Confederates had been manning the wire, watching upstream for the approach of the Federals.

At about midnight on Christmas Eve, at the Vicksburg end of the wire, an Army telegrapher named Philip H. Hall suddenly received an agitated message from a post at Lake Providence, 42 miles to the north. "Great God, Phil," it began, "eighty-one gunboats and transports have passed here tonight." The night was stormy and the river rough. With great difficulty, Hall managed to cross to the east bank; he raced into town and interrupted the Christmas ball being held at a prominent physician's home. Major General Martin Luther Smith, commander of the Vicksburg defenses, listened to the message, paled, and shouted: "The party is at an end!"

At the time, Smith had only 6,000 troops to man the 10-mile line of bluffs along the Yazoo where Sherman's 30,000 Federals were expected to attack. But thanks to the warning—and the fact that Sherman had paused to destroy some railroad tracks at Milliken's Bend, 15 miles north of Vicksburg—Smith was able to muster reinforcements from the Jackson area. About 6,000 men had arrived, with another 13,000 on the way, by the time Sherman drew near on December 26. Sherman landed his men on the south bank of the Yazoo seven miles above its confluence with the Mississippi and four miles northwest of Chickasaw Bluffs.

Sherman advanced slowly over the swampy ground. Not until the morning of December 28 did the Federals approach the foot of the bluffs. There, facing a stretch of bayou and bog with an abatis beyond, they were stopped by a fearsome bombardment from Confederate cannon on the heights above. "The smoke of battle settled thick and heavy over the swamp," Frank D. Mason of the 42nd Ohio recalled, "and through this mist the rising sun shone red and ominous."

All day and through the night, Sherman's men probed the defenses. But the Confederate field commander, Brigadier General Stephen D. Lee, had his forces well prepared, and the Federals got nowhere. Sherman then decided to concentrate his effort on the left. There, in front of one brigade, a narrow causeway crossed the bayou; before another lay a swampy but passable area. Sherman called on the division commander, Brigadier General George Washington Morgan, to attack, adding a less-than-heartening comment: "We will lose 5,000 men before we take Vicksburg, and we may as well lose them here as anywhere else."

Morgan protested that an entire army would not be able to carry the Confederate position. But he obeyed orders, and commanded Brigadier General Francis P. Blair Jr. to push the one brigade across the swamp and Colonel John F. DeCourcy to take the other across the causeway. "My poor brigade!" DeCourcy responded—and then ordered the advance.

Captain William W. Olds of the 42nd Ohio, a regiment in DeCourcy's brigade, described the situation: "The proposed point of attack upon the bluff proved to be the interior of an arc or semicircle, so as the storming brigade advanced it found itself in the center of a converging fire, a flam-

Small Arms for Federal Sailors

Federal warships plying narrow Southern waterways faced a danger that their big guns could do little to prevent — a lightning strike by an enemy boarding party. To guard against this risk, each warship maintained a small arsenal of weapons for close-quarters combat. In times of peril, the weapons were taken from storage and passed out to selected

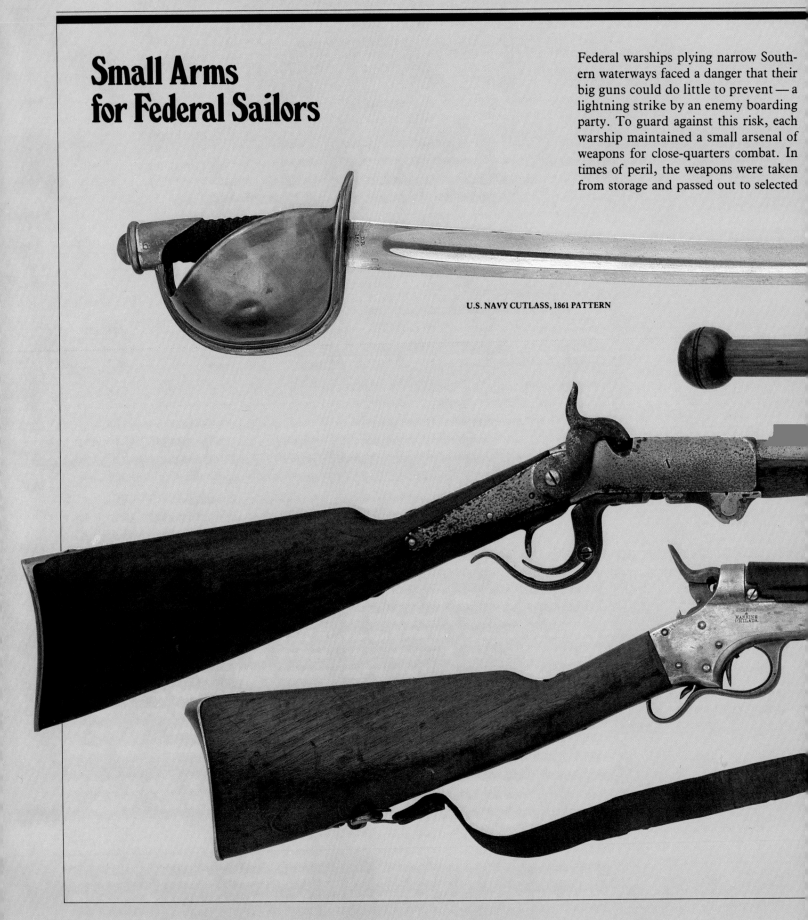

U.S. NAVY CUTLASS, 1861 PATTERN

crewmen. Besides the cutlass — the traditional sailor's weapon for hand-to-hand fighting — a Civil War sailor might also carry a modern, breech-loading carbine, a single-action revolver and a cartridge box. The metal surfaces of the carbines were tinned to resist corrosion. The Sharps & Hankins model shown below came with a leather barrel cover for added protection against water damage.

The menacing battle ax, which dated from the War of 1812, doubled as a tool for cutting away wreckage and downed rigging. For those men whose duties prevented the wearing of such encumbrances, extra weapons were placed in racks at convenient locations throughout the vessel.

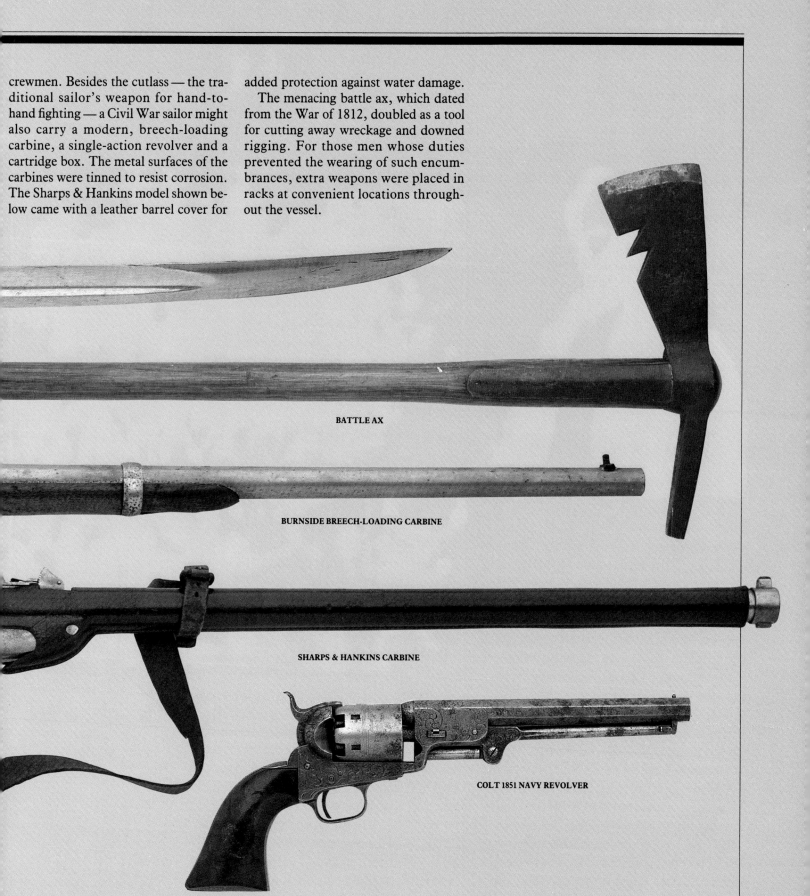

BATTLE AX

BURNSIDE BREECH-LOADING CARBINE

SHARPS & HANKINS CARBINE

COLT 1851 NAVY REVOLVER

MAJOR GENERAL WILLIAM T. SHERMAN

ing hell of shot, shell, shrapnel, canister and minie balls. It would be vain to attempt any description of the noise and confusion of that hour."

Despite the terrain and the murderous fire, both brigades fought their way through the abatis to the foot of the bluff, but there they were pinned down. "Balls came zip-zip into the trees and the ground around us," Captain Olds wrote, "occasionally, thud, a bullet takes some poor fellow and he is carried to the rear."

Ordered forward to support the attack, Brigadier General John M. Thayer's brigade went astray in the swamp. Still, the men of one regiment — the 4th Iowa — found their way to the base of the bluff, where they were halted by a ferocious barrage. The defenders overhead, said Sherman, "held their muskets outside the parapets vertically and fired down." So devastating was the fire that the soldiers had to scoop out protective caves in the bank with their hands.

The Federal attack had failed. "All formations were broken," General Morgan reported. "They were terribly repulsed, but not beaten. There was neither rout nor panic, but our troops fell back slowly and angrily to our own line, halted, re-formed, and, if ordered, would again have rushed to the assault." The men of the 4th Iowa stayed in their burrows under the cliff, shivering in a driving rain, until darkness came. Only then could they safely leave their holes and scur-

This fanciful engraving depicts William Tecumseh Sherman's troops storming Chickasaw Bluffs north of Vicksburg. In reality, the Confederate defenders under Stephen D. Lee stopped the Federals at the base of the bluffs.

BRIGADIER GENERAL STEPHEN D. LEE

ry, one by one, back to their lines. The day had been a calamity. Federal casualties totaled 1,776, Confederate losses 187.

But Sherman was determined to try again the next day. He now intended to attack farther upstream at Haynes' Bluff, the northeastern end of the high ridge along the Yazoo. There the bluffs directly overlooked the river and Confederate fortifications effectively closed the Yazoo to Federal traffic. If Sherman could eliminate those fortifications, his troops could move up the Yazoo, skirt the bluffs and descend on Vicks-

burg from the east, where its defenses were less formidable.

Sherman asked Porter to shift the troops to another landing place upriver for the second attempt. By now the steamboat captains, civilians hired for the expedition, had been thoroughly shaken by the terrors of battle. Sherman wrote: "We had to place sentinels with loaded muskets to insure their remaining at their posts."

Just as Sherman was preparing to resume the attack upstream, the area was blanketed by a fog "so thick and impenetrable," he remarked, "that it was simply impossible to move." Then it began to rain heavily. Looking about him, Sherman noted that the river's high-water mark, visible on the trees, was "ten feet above our heads." If the army stayed it might drown. Reluctantly, Sherman withdrew across the Mississippi to Milliken's Bend.

A few days later, in a letter to his wife, the disconsolate general provided a bleak summation of the recent events: "Well, we have been to Vicksburg, and it was too much for us, and we have backed out." To make his draught more bitter, Sherman at last received the message from Grant ordering that the command be turned over to McClernand, who arrived almost immediately thereafter.

On January 4, 1863, Sherman handed over control of the troops without a protest. Then he confided to McClernand that he had been contemplating trying to redeem something from the Chickasaw Bluffs failure by making an attack on Fort Hindman, on the Arkansas River about 120 miles northwest of Vicksburg. Known to both Federals and Confederates simply as Arkansas Post, Fort Hindman posed a threat to Federal communications on the Mississippi; a Union courier boat on its way down the Mississippi had recently been captured by a force from the fort. Sherman suggested to McClernand that they proceed upstream and attack the Arkansas Post forthwith. McClernand, never one to pass up a chance for glory, quickly agreed.

There was never any question about the outcome. McClernand's force numbered about 30,000 men, the defending troops only 5,000. Even so, the Confederate garrison fought gamely.

On January 11, under heavy shellfire from Porter's gunboats and Federal land batteries, the Confederates defending Fort Hindman managed to stave off an attack on their left by four of Sherman's brigades. Meanwhile, the soldiers of McClernand's XIII Corps advanced on the Confederate right flank and charged the fort, spearheaded by

Brigadier General Stephen Burbridge's men. Although Burbridge's brigade lost 349 men, two of his regiments — the 16th Indiana and 83rd Ohio — succeeded in gaining a foothold atop the parapet.

About 5 p.m., realizing that any further resistance would be pointless, the Confederate commander, Brigadier General Thomas J. Churchill, surrendered Fort Hindman. At a cost of 1,061 casualties, the Federals had captured the entire Confederate garrison, along with 17 cannon, 46,000 rounds of small-arms ammunition, and seven stands of colors.

The victory did little to ease Grant's reservations about McClernand. Grant still believed that the Illinois politician had more rank than ability. McClernand's men disliked him, and his brother officers mistrusted him. Yet while Grant had the authority to remove him, he lacked cause. The command consisted of four corps, with McClernand as senior corps commander over Major Generals Sherman, James B. McPherson and Stephen A. Hurlbut. If Grant remained at his Memphis headquarters and controlled the campaign against Vicksburg from there, as he had intended, the field command would fall to McClernand. That was unthinkable. "Nothing was left, therefore," Grant wrote later, "but to assume the command myself."

On the 29th of January, he traveled downriver to Young's Point, Louisiana — just below Milliken's Bend — where McClernand and Sherman had established their headquarters. On the following day Grant assumed direct command of the army in the field. His troops, excepting Hurlbut's corps, which remained at Memphis, were soon to follow down the Mississippi to the base at

Federal gunboats in the Arkansas River loose a storm of shot and shell on the Confederates' Fort Hindman, also known as Arkansas Post. On shore, columns of infantry under General John McClernand close in to seize the garrison.

Milliken's Bend. The troublesome McClernand was now firmly in hand — at least for the time being.

Farragut had failed, Sherman had failed, and now it was Grant's turn. During the next two and a half months, he would launch no fewer than four amphibious operations aimed at capturing Vicksburg or bypassing it entirely. All were highly unconventional; although he was in a profession that worshipped precedent, Grant was always willing to try something new. He would refer to the four attacks as "experiments," yet he clearly hoped that at least one of them would succeed.

These operations were conducted more or less concurrently at a time when Grant's army might have been expected to go into winter quarters to wait out the bad weather and terrible road conditions of the season. But Grant apparently thought it better to keep his men active, even on somewhat dubious projects, than to relegate them to months of idleness, with the attendant problems of disease and low morale.

The first of the attempts was simply a return to the canal begun by Brigadier General Thomas Williams the previous June, during Farragut's second Vicksburg expedition. The purpose of the canal was to cut

A Soldier's Drawings of the Riverside War

On the cover of his journal, Daniel Allen offers "ten thousands thanks" to whoever might find and return the diary to him or his family in case he lost it. As it happened, Allen eventually returned home safely with his illustrated journal.

For Daniel B. Allen, a former surveyor from Peoria, Illinois, the Vicksburg Campaign was a time of unrelieved misery. Allen enlisted at the age of 39 as a drum major with the 77th Illinois, and soon began to record his woes in a meticulous journal illustrated with sketches of his travels, some of which are shown here.

Allen spent much of the campaign on the Mississippi River aboard what he called a "nasty filthy steamboat," where almost daily, soldiers died from disease. After enduring months of inaction, his regiment joined the battles at Chickasaw Bluffs and Fort Hindman. Allen was horrified by the bursting shells and roaring cannon. But what most deeply troubled him was the havoc wrought by Federal soldiers bent on ravaging the Southern countryside no matter who would suffer. After a raid that destroyed 20 homes of elderly slaves, he wrote, "Alas, how long am I doomed to witness such scenes?"

"I have seen enough of war," he wrote home. "The groans of the wounded and dying are still ringing in my ears." After seven months of anguish and ill health, Allen's wish for relief was granted and he was discharged.

In a scene drawn by Allen on January 5, 1863, ships of the fleet put in for firewood at a plantation north of Chickasaw Bluffs. Allen noted that Federal soldiers stole "everything they could carry off," then "set fire to a large cotton building."

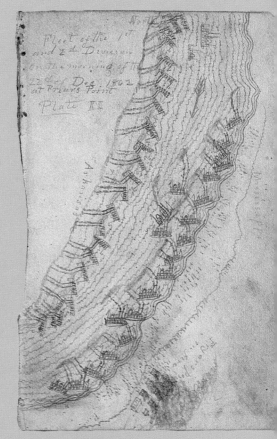

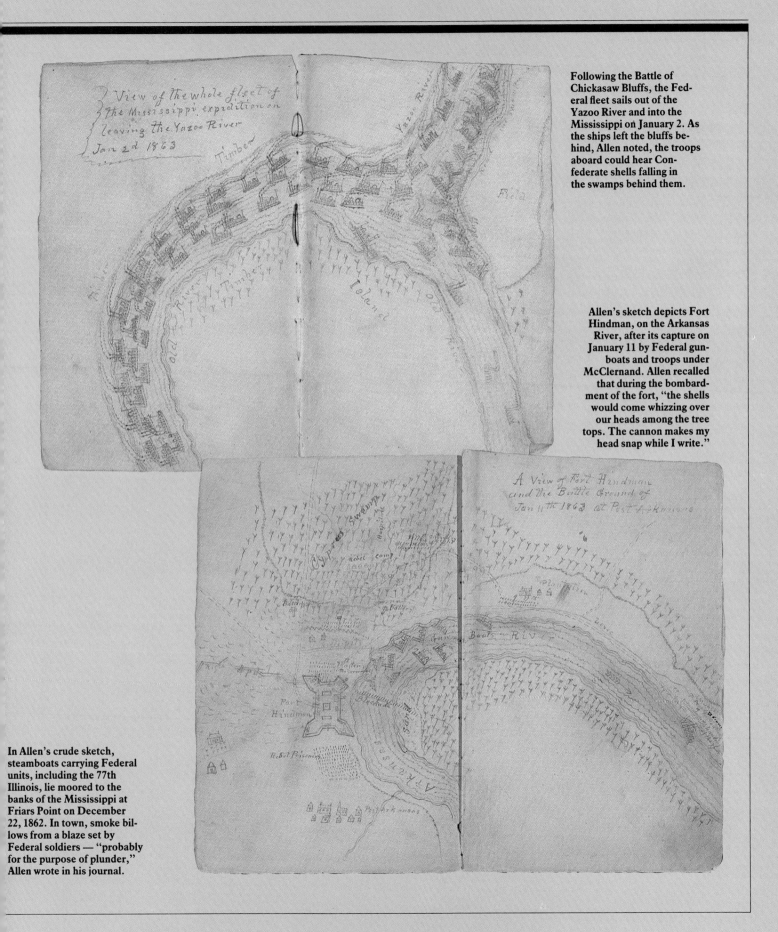

View of the whole fleet of the Mississippi expedition on leaving the Yazoo River Jan 2d 1863

Following the Battle of Chickasaw Bluffs, the Federal fleet sails out of the Yazoo River and into the Mississippi on January 2. As the ships left the bluffs behind, Allen noted, the troops aboard could hear Confederate shells falling in the swamps behind them.

Allen's sketch depicts Fort Hindman, on the Arkansas River, after its capture on January 11 by Federal gunboats and troops under McClernand. Allen recalled that during the bombardment of the fort, "the shells would come whizzing over our heads among the tree tops. The cannon makes my head snap while I write."

In Allen's crude sketch, steamboats carrying Federal units, including the 77th Illinois, lie moored to the banks of the Mississippi at Friars Point on December 22, 1862. In town, smoke billows from a blaze set by Federal soldiers — "probably for the purpose of plunder," Allen wrote in his journal.

across the mile-wide peninsula formed by the horseshoe bend of the Mississippi at Vicksburg and thus bypass the port's defenses. Williams' troops had dug the canal to an average depth of 13 feet and an average width of 18 feet before the project was abandoned.

Grant was truly dubious about the canal, but the resumption of work on it was dictated by the interest of Abraham Lincoln, a man with as strong a predilection for the unconventional as Grant himself. "The President attaches much importance to this," Halleck wired, and Grant obediently started work.

To be useful, the canal had to accommodate vessels with beams as broad as 60 feet and drafts as deep as nine feet. Sherman was given the inglorious assignment of enlarging it.

It was messy work. The January rains were the worst in memory; the river kept rising, threatening not only the labor but the laborers. Sherman was living in a house on high ground that could be reached only by planks laid from a levee over surrounding water, and the men were living on the levee itself, trying to stay dry. "Rain, rain," Sherman wrote his wife, "water above, below and all around. I have been doused under water by my horse falling in a hole, and got a good ducking yesterday walking where a horse could not go." In all that dampness insects thrived, and one soldier complained that the air was simply "a saturated solution of gnats."

There were those — Sherman included — who doubted that the canal would ever serve its intended purpose. The upstream end was situated on an eddy of the Mississippi, and the river was not likely to flow readily into

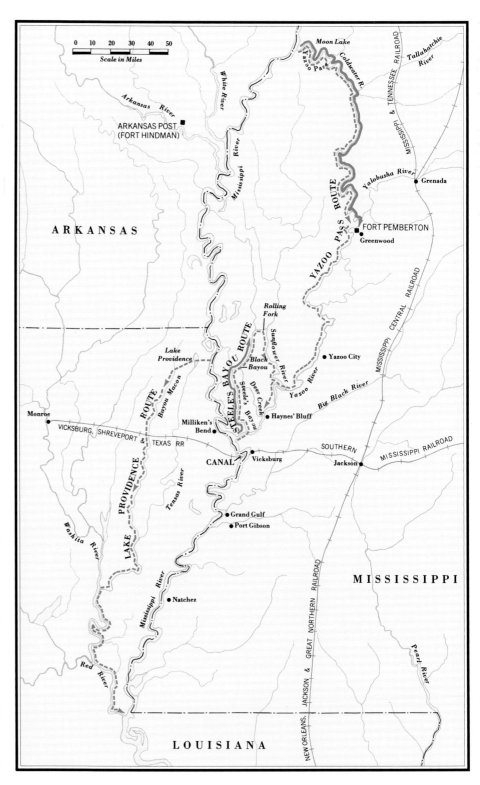

the canal. The downstream end looked right into the muzzles of Confederate guns across the river; the first boat to go through would surely be blown out of the water. "The canal won't do," Sherman wrote his wife. It was "a pure waste of human labor."

Still, the President apparently wanted it, and the army did its best. The shape of the canal's mouth was changed to capture more of the reluctant river, dredge boats were brought in to speed the digging, and the canal's dimensions were enlarged as ordered. Then, just as plans were made to cut the temporary dam at the upstream end and let the Mississippi in, the river arrived unbidden. There was a new onslaught of torrential rains, the water rose, and the dam gave way. The Mississippi rushed through, but instead of scouring out the canal as expected, it overflowed the banks, flooding the surrounding fields and threatening the soldiers on the levees. That did not end the trouble: When the water had subsided and the Federal crews returned to the canal, the Confederates began shooting at the dredges from across the river.

That was enough for Grant. He called off the project. The canal might someday be used by boats at night, he said, but that was all.

By now, Grant's attention was fastened on a different way of skirting Vicksburg. On the Louisiana side of the river about 40 miles north of Vicksburg lay a body of water known as Lake Providence. At one time, it had been a bend of the Mississippi, but the river had changed course, and now it lay a mile inland. However, the lake could be connected again — and Grant estimated that the project would involve less than a quarter of the effort the canal had required. Once

in Lake Providence, Union vessels might be able to pick their way down a chain of southward-flowing waterways to the Red River, which in turn would lead them back to the Mississippi below Vicksburg. Grant estimated the distance from entry to exit at something more than 470 miles, and at the far end the traveler would be 250 river miles south of Vicksburg. The success of this operation might also bring the Federals closer to eliminating another Confederate river stronghold, the little Louisiana town of Port Hudson.

This well-fortified, bluff-top town was situated about 50 miles south of the exit to Grant's projected waterway, and just north of Baton Rouge, dominating the Mississippi at that point just as Vicksburg did to the north. Both strongholds would have to be conquered before the Union could open up the river.

In October 1862, Major General Nathaniel P. Banks had been placed in command of Federal forces at New Orleans with orders to help clear the river northward. He and Grant had been instructed to cooperate in their campaigns. Thus far, Grant had focused on Vicksburg, while Banks had concentrated on Port Hudson. The long journey from Lake Providence to the Red River would be worthwhile, Grant thought, if their two forces could then join in attacking the Confederate garrison at Port Hudson and move together on Vicksburg.

General McPherson, one of Grant's corps commanders and a man with a wealth of engineering experience, was given the assignment of opening the intervening waterways. With great difficulty, a 30-ton steamer was transported overland from the Mississippi to Lake Providence for use in reconnaissance. McPherson established his headquarters aboard this vessel.

The waterway south from Lake Providence led through a swamp, and McPherson set his men to work cutting a channel through this boggy area. Immense cypress trees barred the way; they had to be cut down and removed without leaving stumps underwater to block the passage of transports. In order to get at the stumps after the trees were cut down, McPherson's men invented an underwater saw. They mounted a circular saw on a shaft that could be lowered from a floating platform. When the blade was in position at the required depth, men on the platform turned the shaft and the saw bit into the stump. The new tool worked admirably; once the stumps were severed, they bobbed to the surface for disposal. But it was obvious that the job was going to be long and hard. And when the work had dragged on for two months without much progress, Grant concluded that the distance was too great and the obstacles too forbidding.

On the east bank of the Mississippi, however, another network of waterways — this one leading directly to Vicksburg — was proving somewhat more promising. For many years before the War, much of the river traffic coming down the Mississippi had turned off 350 miles north of Vicksburg, into a waterway called the Yazoo Pass, and had proceeded through various deepwater streams to trade at ports on the upper Yazoo River, about 80 miles east of the Mississippi. New Orleans-bound boats had only to follow the Yazoo south to regain the Mississippi just above Vicksburg. If Federal forces could descend the Yazoo and land north of Haynes' Bluff, Grant realized, they would be able to bypass the formidable Confeder-

ate river defenses there and attack Vicksburg from the east.

The problem was how to get into the Yazoo Pass. In the mid-1850s, the state of Mississippi had constructed a levee 100 feet thick and 18 feet high across the entrance to the pass. Mississippians had thus lost a useful waterway, but they had gained much-needed protection from frequent floods. That levee would have to be cut in order to give Federal forces access to the old watercourse. They could then move swiftly to the Yazoo River.

The proposed route was scouted by a young West Pointer on Grant's staff, Lieutenant Colonel James H. Wilson, and pronounced entirely feasible. The Confederates under General Pemberton were expected to put up little resistance, and Grant himself predicted that the attempt to move on Vicksburg through the Yazoo Pass would be "a perfect success."

On February 2, Wilson set off an explosion under the levee to let the Mississippi into the pass. It was a spectacular sight: The difference in water levels was nine feet, and the flood-swollen river poured through in a solid wall. The rushing waters quickly carved an opening 200 feet wide in the levee, and several days later the river was still flowing swiftly through the gap.

The current was too strong for safe navigation, but the Federal forces could wait no longer. On the 7th of February, 4,500 Union soldiers — a number of whom had been transported 350 miles upriver from the Vicksburg area so that they could make this 350-mile voyage back down again — boarded small vessels and began venturing into the gap. They were headed toward Moon Lake, another former bend of the Mississippi

now located about a mile from the river.

Captain Samuel Byers of the 5th Iowa Infantry was on a little steamer that entered the pass with its engines running in reverse to give its captain some semblance of control. The current grabbed the craft and whirled it around, Byers recalled, "like a toy skiff in a washtub," flinging it through the pass amid floating logs and debris, and slamming it into trees. "In ten minutes," wrote Byers, "the rushing torrent had carried us, backward, down into the little lake. Not a soul of the five hundred on board the boat in this crazy ride was lost. Once in the lake we stopped, and with amazement watched other boats, crowded with soldiers, also drift into the whirl and be swept down the pass. It was luck, not management, that half the little army was not drowned."

The Federal commanders had hoped to catch the Confederates napping, but once again Pemberton had shown that he was an able soldier. The Federal vessels had scarcely entered the flooded streams when they began to encounter obstacles put there by Confederate work parties. Huge trees, some of them four feet in diameter and weighing 20 tons, had been felled across the channel. The Federals faced stretches, wrote Lieutenant Colonel Wilson, where "for miles there was an entanglement so thick the troops could cross it from bank to bank."

Removing such barricades appeared at first glance to be a major engineering operation, but in fact it was achieved in the simplest way possible. Soldiers dragged the trees out of the way with rope cables, 500 men to the cable. They appear to have enjoyed the work; Admiral Porter related that the troops entertained themselves with "jolly songs."

Other obstacles impeded progress. Some of the river bends were so tight that the vessels were unable to maneuver past them under their own power and had to be hauled around them with hawsers. The trees were so thick in places that their branches interlocked over the channels to form woody tunnels. The troop carriers were regular river boats, with high, fragile superstructures and towering smokestacks that were extremely vulnerable to such overhead obstructions. "Steamers could not pass," wrote Admiral Porter, "without having their smoke-pipes knocked down and all their boats and upper works swept away." By the second day, he went on, "the vessels were so torn to pieces that no more harm could be done to them — they had hulls and engines left and that had to suffice."

With all this, the expedition's forward movement was excruciatingly sluggish. "The men were rewarded after four days of terrible labor," said Porter, "by getting forty miles on their journey."

Even fewer rewards lay ahead. Just as the Federal force reached a point where another stream, the Yalobusha, enters the main river — the men received an unpleasant surprise. There the Confederates had blocked the river by sinking old ships in the channel and had hastily constructed a fortification of cotton bales and sandbags. Cannon had been mounted over the improvised parapets, and 1,500 soldiers were manning the fort under the command of Major General William W. Loring.

The Confederates had named this strongpoint Fort Pemberton, after the general, and however crude it appeared, it was in fact a formidable obstacle. It was located at a passage so narrow that only one or two boats could approach at one time, and it was surrounded by terrain so marshy that no foot soldiers could get to it at all. It also was half hidden by a bend. Thus the Union invaders, creeping down the river, would come upon it unexpectedly.

The Federal naval force was led by Lieutenant Commander Watson Smith, and he was in no condition to deal with surprises. A nervous and cautious officer, Smith had been showing signs of strain for some time. His progress down the river had been painfully slow. If his gunboats had moved faster, they might have taken Fort Pemberton before its defenders were ready. But Smith had anxiously held the whole force to the speed of the transports, and had grown more and more worried as his force moved deeper into enemy territory. Suddenly confronted by Fort Pemberton, Smith stopped all his boats and spent several days summoning his nerve. Then he sent two of his gunboats forward.

They were instantly blasted by the Confederates, and had great difficulty bringing their own guns to bear. Smith pulled the boats back, appalled. He was now displaying all the indications of what Porter later called "aberration of mind." Among other things, he was growing incoherent, shouting orders to his men that no one could understand. On March 17, Smith asked to be relieved. He was replaced by Lieutenant Commander James P. Foster.

Two more efforts were made to get the gunboats past Fort Pemberton. Both were met by furious gunfire from the fort. "Give them blizzards, boys!" cried General Loring, who would be known to the Confederates ever after as "Old Blizzards." The Federals escaped with relatively few casualties, but they were checked. At last, the expedition turned around and headed back on the long journey to Yazoo Pass, which it had entered so hopefully eight weeks before. Its leaders were greatly downcast at this anticlimactic outcome, but the enlisted men and junior officers thought it had turned out just fine. "The picturesque farce was ended," wrote Samuel Byers cheerfully. "We know nothing of what the generals thought of this fiasco, but we private soldiers had great fun, and the long stay on the boats had been a rest from hard campaigning."

Weeks before, while Grant's bayou experiments were proceeding apace, Admiral Porter had attempted a strike of his own against the Confederates. Vicksburg was still receiving substantial supplies from the West via the Red River, whose entrance to the Mississippi north of Port Hudson lay in that 250-mile stretch still controlled by the Confederates. On February 3, under orders from Porter to put a stop to the Red River commerce, the youthful Colonel Charles Rivers Ellet headed south past the Vicksburg batteries in the *Queen of the West,* the ram his father had commanded. On the way past the Vicksburg docks, Ellet spotted the steamer *City of Vicksburg* moored there, and braved the batteries to ram her and set her afire with flaming balls of turpentine-soaked cotton. The *Queen of the West* sustained some damage, but not enough to prevent Ellet from proceeding down the Mississippi.

The next day the *Queen* headed up the Red River and wreaked havoc on Confederate shipping. Ellet captured three steamers, a number of army officers and vast quantities of supplies. On the following day, he claimed two more river boats and their cargo. Then he moved on with his little fleet to attack the

Confederate fortifications at Gordon's Point, about 85 miles up the river.

There his luck deserted him. Just as the Confederate guns opened up on the *Queen of the West,* she ran aground (misdirected, her crew would claim, by a treacherous pilot). There were wounded men aboard the *Queen* who could not be moved, so Ellet was unable to destroy his vessel. Instead he escaped on one of the captured steamers, leaving the *Queen* and her injured crew members to the mercies of the Confederates. They quickly made the most of their prize, repairing the *Queen* and returning her to action. Later that February, along with a second ram and two Confederate gunboats, she encountered another Federal vessel sent down by Porter — the *Indianola* — just below Vicksburg. A vio-

lent melee ensued, and the *Indianola* was so badly damaged that she had to be beached by her crew, who then surrendered.

The Union river fleet had paid dearly for its Red River depredations, and Admiral Porter was momentarily taken aback. But Porter was never at a loss for long. The admiral was a man with both admirers and detractors: Grant thought highly of him, but Secretary of War Stanton labeled him a "gasbag." The journalist Sylvanus Cadwallader fairly sputtered when he wrote about Porter, calling him "by all odds the greatest humbug of the war." But what Porter did next suggested that he was an ingenious and irrepressible man with a sense of humor.

He put his sailors to work on an old coal barge attached to the fleet. They extended its

The U.S. Navy's *Queen of the West,* commanded by 19-year-old Colonel Charles Rivers Ellet, fires on the Confederate gunboat *City of Vicksburg,* moored at Vicksburg. During a 12-day raid, Ellet destroyed $200,000 worth of food and cotton in attacks on steamers supplying the city.

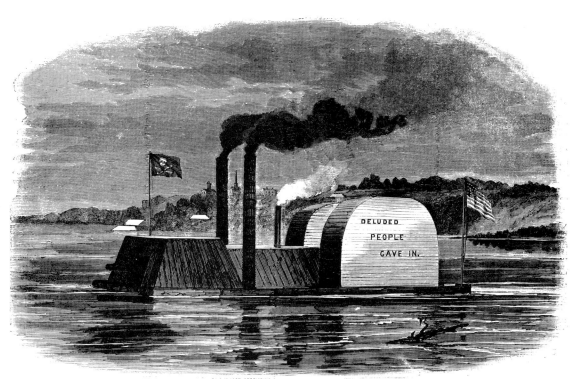

Adrift in the Mississippi, a counterfeit Union gunboat sweeps past Vicksburg on the night of February 25, 1863. The vessel, made by transforming an old barge with scrap wood, canvas and tar, thoroughly fooled the Confederates. Admiral Porter boasted, "Never did the batteries of Vicksburg open with such a din."

length to 300 feet with a raft of logs, built a deckhouse of canvas atop it, constructed two phony smokestacks out of barrels, and furnished the dummy vessel with a number of imposing-looking log cannon. When the task was done, the converted barge, built at a cost of $8.63, resembled a huge gunboat. Porter provided the vessel with smoke by lighting pitch fires in iron pots under the false smokestacks, and set it adrift above Vicksburg.

Porter hoped that his fraudulent warship would divert the Confederates from their attempt to salvage the beached *Indianola*. The results must have exceeded his fondest wishes. As the great apparition floated majestically down the river, the Vicksburg guns opened up on her. But the shot and shell had no apparent effect, and she proceeded disdainfully on her way. Below the town she encountered the *Queen of the West*, en route to Vicksburg to get a pump for the crew that was working frantically to salvage the *Indianola*. The Confederates aboard the *Queen* took one look at the monster bearing down on them and instantly turned tail. As they sped south, they alerted the three other vessels that had helped attack the

Indianola, and all four hastened to safety.

Left behind, the salvage crew aboard the *Indianola* stared as Porter's dummy swept down the river, headed directly for them. Then the barge struck a sandbar and halted, dark and forbidding. The Confederate salvagers endured the looming, fearsome presence as long as they could, then they set fire to the *Indianola* and took to their boats.

The next day, the big black apparition was still sitting in midriver, doing nothing, and a party of Confederates gingerly set forth to get a closer look. As they neared, they could see Porter's dummy for what it was. At her bow flew the pirate ensign, the skull and crossbones. On the canvas housings over her nonexistent sidewheels was printed a message in yard-high letters. "Deluded people," it read, "cave in!"

The dummy-ship escapade was scarcely over when Porter found himself involved in the fourth of the bayou experiments. Midway in the course of the Yazoo Pass expedition, Grant had begun to worry that the waterborne troops heading down the Yazoo might become trapped, and he asked for an exploration of the waterways at the lower end of

the river, in case he had to mount a rescue mission. Soon afterward, Porter invited Grant for a boat ride. By then all danger to the Yazoo Pass participants appeared over, but Porter thought he might have discovered a new way into Vicksburg.

They started up the Yazoo on board Porter's flagship, the *Black Hawk*. The river was in flood, not only because of the incessant rains but also because of the millions of gallons of the Mississippi that had been let in at the Yazoo Pass. Suddenly, as they passed a tree-lined bank downriver from Haynes' Bluff, Porter called for a hard turn to port. The vessel wheeled left, and the astonished Grant found himself sailing sedately through the woods. There were trees on all sides; leafy boughs were interlaced overhead. The water's depth at this point was 15 feet; under the *Black Hawk* ran a road that had once carried cotton to the river. Much of the surrounding forest was similarly flooded, Porter pointed out. Though strips of high ground laced the inundated areas, a boat could go almost anywhere.

Soon they were northbound in a waterway called Steele's Bayou. It linked up eventually, Porter explained, with a channel called Black Bayou and then with another known as Deer Creek. Both of these also extended northward. Branching off to the east from Deer Creek was Rolling Fork, and Rolling Fork connected in turn with the Sunflower River. The Sunflower headed back south and ultimately emptied into the Yazoo. It was a zany route. A vessel following it would take five waterways and would travel 200 miles to wind up only 20 miles northeast of where it had started. But in the process it would outflank the Chickasaw Bluffs and Haynes' Bluff defenses north of Vicksburg

and carry troops into position for an attack on the city from the rear.

Porter had explored only as far as Deer Creek, but he considered the entire route navigable. Grant was captivated. He authorized the expedition as soon as he was back at his headquarters that night. Porter wanted to lead the Steele's Bayou venture himself. Grant approved, and ordered Sherman and 10,000 men to accompany him.

It was a madcap adventure almost from the start. For eight or 10 miles the trees were far enough apart so that the expedition's 11 ships could steam through them in a straight line. As Porter noted, the vessels were "pushing their way through the long, wide lane in the woods without touching on either side."

Then the forest thickened, and 100-year-old trees barred the way. But the ground around their root systems had been softened by water, and as Porter's vessels nudged the trunks, the trees slowly fell over. The watercourse grew narrower; at one point it consisted of an old canal that was almost exactly the width of the Federal gunboats. After a while the channel began to twist: Porter recalled that at one time he could look into the woods and see five boats, each following another bow-to-stern, but all pointing in different directions as they conformed to the winding path of the stream. Occasionally a gunboat would become jammed between two trees and would have to be chopped free.

To add to the Navy's problems, Porter wrote, "the dead trees were full of vermin of all sorts." The area's wildlife had been driven into the trees by the flood waters, and as the vessels brushed by underneath there was a steady deluge of creatures. Rats, mice, snakes, raccoons, cockroaches and liz-

ards came raining down on the decks and were promptly swept overboard by sailors armed with brooms.

Suddenly Porter and his men ran into real trouble. Within sight of the Sunflower River, they were halted by a tangle of willow so thick that no boat could penetrate it. While they were trying to extricate themselves, they spotted a vessel landing a force of gray-clad men on a levee along the Sunflower.

Porter, mindful of Watson Smith's laggard ways, had not let himself be slowed by the troop transports; by this time Sherman and his infantrymen were many miles to the rear. All at once, Confederate artillery fire began to descend on Porter's ships. Hastily,

the admiral scrawled a note to Sherman and entrusted it to a local black man who knew the way. "Dear Sherman," the message read. "Hurry up, for Heaven's sake. I never knew how helpless an ironclad could be steaming around through the woods without an army to back her."

Sherman put a rescue party aboard a troop transport and a coal barge that had to be towed through the bayous by tug. It was not long, he wrote, before trees had carried away the tug's superstructure: "pilot house, smokestacks and everything above deck." By nightfall the Federal soldiers had gone as far as they could by boat, so they clambered out and made their way through canebrakes

The Union transport *Silver Wave* picks its way up Steele's Bayou during Grant's last attempt to bypass Vicksburg's defenses. "The ironclads push their way along unharmed," reported General Sherman, "but the trees and overhanging limbs tear the wooden boats all to pieces."

on fingers of high ground. Late at night they slept briefly, then rose at dawn to continue on their way.

By the time the rescue party reached the beleaguered boats, Porter had begun to retreat under fierce enemy fire. He had covered his gunwales with slime to ward off boarders, and was preparing for the worst. "I doubt," said Sherman, "if he was ever more glad to meet a friend than he was to meet me." The attacking Confederates had chopped down trees across the route to the Sunflower, and they were just beginning to do the same behind Porter to close the trap when Sherman's troops arrived.

Backed by the Federal infantry, Porter's boats continued their retreat. The craft had no room to turn around, so their rudders were unshipped to keep them from snagging, and with the utmost care the vessels were backed out of the maze of bayous. Their rearward progress was noisily observed by the Federal infantrymen on the banks. "Where's all your masts and sails?" one soldier called out innocently. "By the Widow Perkins," another taunted, "if Johnny Reb hasn't taken their rudders away and set them adrift!"

Another bayou experiment had failed. Confederates who had captured a Federal officer asked him what Grant thought he was doing: "Hasn't the old fool tried this ditching and flanking five times already?"

"Yes," replied the prisoner, "but he has thirty-seven more plans in his pocket."

The fact was, Grant had only one more plan in his pocket. With the conclusion of the Steele's Bayou expedition the initial phase of the Vicksburg Campaign was over. It was now early April; the weather was growing warmer, and the time for experiments was past. For weeks, while the bayou adventures had been under way, Grant had been spending long hours at his headquarters near Milliken's Bend, puffing his cigar and planning.

The best approach to Vicksburg, without doubt, had been the one he had begun back in December — down the Mississippi Central Railroad to the town's rear. But to try it again, Grant would first have to move his army from its camps on the Mississippi's west bank back up the river to Memphis, the terminus of the railroad. That movement was manifestly ill-advised — not because of any considerations of strategy or geography, but for political reasons.

Civilian morale in the North had never been lower. In the East there had been no Union victory since the costly triumph at Antietam the previous September, and there had been one terrible, bloody defeat, at Fredericksburg. In the West, Federal forces had managed only a few successes since Shiloh. All of Grant's experiments had been recognized in Washington as failures, and he was coming under increasing press criticism. To seem to be retreating toward Memphis now would be out of the question. It was entirely possible that such a move would force Lincoln's hand and cost Grant his job.

That left only one approach. Grant must take his army still farther down the west bank of the Mississippi, well below Vicksburg. Then he must cross over and attack from the south. This time he would not send just a division or a corps; he would move with three corps, risking everything on one throw of the dice. And he would command the operation himself.

A Beachhead on the East Bank

"We are out of ammunition. They outnumber us trebly. My whole force is engaged. The men act nobly, but the odds are overpowering."

BRIGADIER GENERAL JOHN S. BOWEN, C.S.A., AT PORT GIBSON

Grant's new plan was bold to the point of rashness. Facing an enemy that outnumbered him almost 2 to 1, he was proposing to carry out an amphibious landing with no certain way of supplying his army after it was ashore, and with no practical route of retreat open to him if he was defeated. Sherman, his trusted friend, opposed the plan fiercely, as did McPherson, another of Grant's corps commanders.

General John Pemberton's Confederate army, in and around Vicksburg, totaled approximately 60,000 men. Grant had about 33,000 available for the landing. Of those, fewer than one third could be carried by the Federal transport fleet in the first wave. If Pemberton met the Federal assault at the shore with his full strength, Grant would face catastrophe. Any attempt to reembark the landing force under fire invited wholesale slaughter. The only other possible avenue of escape open to him would be a long march through Confederate territory to one of the distant Federal bases — perhaps Corinth, or Memphis, or Baton Rouge.

A more immediate problem for Grant was moving his army 40 miles from Milliken's Bend to a base at New Carthage, on the west bank of the Mississippi 20 miles below Vicksburg. He hoped to transfer most of the troops and matériel overland down the west bank and then strike before Pemberton realized what was happening. But once again the wet weather was Grant's implacable enemy. Some of the roads were flooded, and all were deep in mud. Federal troops marching through the mire to New Carthage had to improvise bridges over many of the swollen bayous. Supply wagons bogged down hopelessly. The men of McClernand's XIII Corps cleared a water route through the bayous, but perversely, the level of the Mississippi suddenly fell, and not even shallow-draft vessels could get through the waterway.

The roads, meanwhile, remained as wet as ever. The transfer of the army down the west bank was progressing at a snail's pace. If Grant hoped to launch his offensive quickly, at least some of the troops and the bulk of the supplies would have to be ferried down the Mississippi past the dangerous Vicksburg batteries.

It fell to Porter's gunboats to escort the first shipment past the Confederate guns to New Carthage. Porter chose the night of April 16 for the run. Darkness cloaked the river as Grant, accompanied by his visiting wife and two sons, watched tensely from his headquarters steamer, anchored upstream out of range of the Confederate batteries. Sherman awaited the outcome aboard a boat below the town.

The 12 vessels of the convoy started quietly downstream, their exhausts vented into the paddle-wheel housings to muffle the noise and reduce the chance of detection. To assure silence, Porter had even ordered his crews to leave ashore all pets, along with the poultry carried by some boats' crews

The battle flag carried at Port Gibson by the 15th Northwest Arkansas Volunteers bears the names of four earlier engagements in which the Confederate regiment took part. The flag was captured at Port Gibson by a private of the 18th Indiana.

to provide fresh food. The captains of the convoy were told to steer a little off to one side of the vessel ahead, so that if a craft was hit, the vessel behind it could pass without slowing down. To afford some protection from shot and shell, many crews had stacked cotton and hay bales, grain sacks and logs on deck; others had lashed coal barges to the sides of their vessels. Belowdecks, teams of men stood ready with cotton wads and gunny sacks to plug any shell holes below the water line.

That night many of the people of Vicksburg, as well as Pemberton's senior officers, were attending a grand ball. Porter, made aware of the gala event by informants, hoped that the party would so preoccupy the enemy that they would not notice the passage of his little fleet. But the Confederate pickets, patrolling the river in skiffs, were alert. They spotted the spectral shadows in the Mississippi almost immediately and sounded the alarm. The ball came to a hasty end and sol-

diers hurried to their posts. From atop the bluffs the batteries opened up.

In an act of great courage, some of the Confederate pickets rowed their skiffs across the river under fire from both sides, landed in Union-held De Soto, and set ablaze several buildings to light up the night. Meanwhile, the defenders of Vicksburg were igniting barrels of pitch on the east bank. Suddenly the whole river was illuminated and the Federal vessels were clearly visible in midstream. "The river," recalled Grant's 12-year-old son, Fred, "was lighted up as if by sunlight."

Captain Byers, the Iowan who in February had made the wild voyage through the Yazoo Pass, was aboard one of the transports, and he later reconstructed the scene. "We see the people in the streets of the town running and gesticulating as if all were mad," he wrote. "Their men at the batteries load and fire and yell as if every shot sunk a steamboat. On the west side of the river the lagoons and the canebrake look weird and dangerous. The sky above is black, lighted only by sparks from the burning houses. Down on the river it is a sheet of flame. One of the steamers and a few of the barges have caught fire and are burning up, the men escaping in lifeboats and by swimming to the western shore." Byers concluded: "It was as if hell itself were loose that night on the Mississippi River."

The passage of the fleet was agonizingly slow: From first to last it took two and a half hours. But when it was over, only those few vessels Byers had seen burning — one transport and a couple of barges — had been lost. Grant's plan was successfully launched.

At New Carthage, Sherman greeted each boat as it arrived. When Porter's flagship appeared, Sherman went aboard and said cheerfully to the admiral: "You are more at home here than you were in the ditches grounding on willow trees."

Sherman was even more pleased at something that occurred a week later, when six more Federal ships attempted to run the Vicksburg defenses. All but one vessel made it — and on board that one were three newspaper reporters. Sherman had nursed a black hatred of the press since the early days of the War, when he had been called crazy in print. His vendetta was renowned in the Army of the Tennessee. Now three "dirty newspaper scribblers," as Sherman termed reporters, had apparently been lost when the transport went down. He could scarcely contain himself. "We'll have dispatches now from hell before breakfast," he gleefully wrote.

Sherman must have been disappointed to learn that the correspondents had not drowned after all, but had merely been captured. One of them was quickly released; the other two were held prisoner for 19 months before they escaped and made their way back to the North.

After the fleet arrived at New Carthage, Sherman returned to Milliken's Bend, where his XV Corps remained on watch, ready to strike at Vicksburg's upriver defenses if Pemberton left them unguarded. Grant's other two corps were now assembling at New Carthage to prepare for the landing.

Although he knew that something was up, Pemberton was still not sure where Grant's main force was headed. As recently as April 11 — five days before Porter's vessels first ran the batteries — Pemberton had notified his superiors that Grant seemed to have given up his designs on Vicksburg and had started north. Pemberton had even detached

Rear Admiral David Dixon Porter, a controversial officer who preferred to operate alone, nevertheless teamed in perfect harmony with Grant. When Grant asked him to run his boats past Vicksburg's guns, Porter complied eagerly. "So confident was I of General Grant's ability to carry out his plans," he wrote later, "that I never hesitated."

some troops for service elsewhere. Porter's exploit had certainly disabused him of the notion that the Federals were moving upriver, but he was still uncertain where the next blow would fall.

Now all of Grant's plans depended on keeping Pemberton confused. For a landing site on the east bank, Grant had chosen a place called Grand Gulf, 20 miles downriver from New Carthage. Grand Gulf offered plenty of dry ground for the troops, and from there they could march to the northwest and flank Vicksburg. But Grant was determined to mask his intentions until it was too late for Pemberton to react effectively.

The obvious course was to mount a series of diversionary actions. With masterful guile, Grant sent a division off to distract the

Despite a fierce bombardme
gunboats and transports of Porte
fleet steam past Vicksburg
April 16, 1863. In the foregrou
a boat carrying General Shermar
being rowed out to greet Admi
Porter on his flagship, the *Bent*

Confederates at Greenville, on the east bank of the Mississippi 100 miles north of Vicksburg. He also dispatched a division of McPherson's corps from Lake Providence to join Sherman at Young's Point, northwest of Vicksburg. By far the most important of these feints was a large cavalry raid south from La Grange, Tennessee, through central Mississippi. The operation would go down in history simply as Grierson's Raid.

Colonel Benjamin H. Grierson may have been the Union Army's most improbable cavalry leader. He had hated horses since the age of eight, when he was kicked and badly hurt by a pony, and he had objected vigor-ously when he was assigned to the 6th Illinois Cavalry in 1861. He had, in fact, protested to none other than General Halleck, who had brushed him off with the comment that he looked "active and wiry enough" to become a cavalryman.

What is more, Grierson was something of a novice in military matters; in April 1863 he had only 18 months of service behind him. He was really a musician — a composer, arranger, pianist, flutist, drummer and guitarist who had been making an uncertain living as a music teacher when the War started. On patrols, he entertained himself and those of his men within earshot by strumming away on a jew's-harp as they rode along.

For all his unlikely background, Grierson quickly earned a reputation as a superb cavalry leader — "the best cavalry officer I have yet had," Sherman had told Grant the previous December. Impressed, the commanding general had picked Grierson to lead this critical raid through the enemy heartland. He would be riding at the head of the 1,700 cavalrymen of the 2nd Iowa and the 6th and 7th Illinois, accompanied by a battery of horse artillery.

His orders were of the most general sort. He was to ride south from La Grange into Mississippi, following a route between the state's two north-south railroads: the Mississippi Central and the Mobile & Ohio. En route, he was to cut both of those lines and sever the even more important Southern Mississippi Railroad, which ran from Vicksburg through Jackson and on east, tying together the eastern and western halves of the Confederacy.

Grierson had also been instructed to disrupt enemy communications elsewhere, destroy any supplies he might come upon, and make as much mischief as possible while deceiving the Confederates about the actual size and identity of his force. Presumably, he would return to La Grange, probably by way of Alabama.

The troopers who rode out of La Grange behind Benjamin Grierson on the morning of April 17 knew only that they were off on a lengthy mission, for they had been ordered to draw five-days' rations. They welcomed this break from their usual routine.

In the first stages of the journey, Grierson's troopers brushed against small detachments of Confederate soldiers and militiamen. The raiders fired a few rounds and took a few prisoners, most of whom were later paroled. More significantly, Grierson's men stirred up the Confederate cavalry.

The cavalry commander in northeastern Mississippi, a 29-year-old lieutenant colonel named Clark R. Barteau, had only about 500 men, but he had plenty of gumption, and he moved swiftly to intercept Grierson's force. Grierson, though, was a wily adversary. On the fourth day out of La Grange, he weeded out all the ailing and injured troopers. This group of more than 150 men — dubbed the Quinine Brigade by their comrades — then started back north, taking care as they went to obliterate a stretch of the southbound hoofprints of the main force. Barteau, in hot pursuit of the raiders, came across the northbound tracks and slowed down. By the time he figured out that the Federals were playing games, he was 10 hours behind Grierson.

On the next day, April 21, Grierson ordered the 2nd Iowa Cavalry under Colonel Edward Hatch to split off and move toward the Confederate base at Columbus, Mississippi, a day's ride to the east; from there Hatch was to head back to La Grange, 175 miles to the north. Hatch's diversion was intended to rouse the countryside and make it appear once again that the entire force was riding homeward. This time, Barteau, now only three hours behind Grierson, swallowed the bait. He went after Hatch, and soon caught up with him. A brisk skirmish ensued. Hatch outnumbered Barteau by 200 men, but he chose a fighting retreat. He believed, he said later, that "it was important to divert the enemy's cavalry from Colonel Grierson." In this he was completely successful. As Hatch moved northward, harried by Barteau, Grierson was proceeding unhampered toward the vital Southern Mississippi Railroad.

Benjamin H. Grierson, a colonel in the Federal cavalry, was a peacetime music teacher who much preferred playing his jew's-harp to riding a horse. But the 16-day raid he led through enemy territory from La Grange, Tennessee, to Baton Rouge, guided only by a pocket map and a small compass, confounded the defenders of Vicksburg and gave the Union a hero on horseback.

Ranging out ahead of the brigade was a contingent of scouts who engaged in the riskiest of deceptions: They dressed as Confederate irregulars, which made them subject to execution as spies if they were captured. These men, known to their fellow cavalrymen as the Butternut Guerrillas, checked out all towns before the main Federal force arrived and attempted to secure vital bridges before they could be destroyed. The scouts also kept a sharp eye out for food and forage — it was now necessary for them to live off the land.

On April 22, the sixth day of the adventure, Colonel Grierson once again detached a unit to sow confusion off to one side of his route. This time he sent Company B of the 7th Illinois Cavalry, 35 men under Captain Henry C. Forbes, to the town of Macon on the Mobile & Ohio Railroad to cut the telegraph lines there.

While Forbes was raising alarms in and around Macon, Grierson's troopers, weary and dusty but still enjoying themselves thoroughly, trotted into the town of Newton Station on April 24. The raiders were now about 200 miles deep in enemy country and about 100 miles directly east of Vicksburg, and they had reached the Southern Mississippi Railroad.

The Butternut Guerrillas had discovered that two trains, one westbound and one eastbound, were due in at any moment. The first of them, a freight train headed west, arrived at almost exactly the same time as Grierson's lead battalion. When the train puffed noisily onto a siding to let the second train pass, the cavalrymen swarmed all over it.

They could scarcely have gained a more welcome prize: It was carrying ordnance and commissary supplies to Vicksburg. Minutes later, the eastbound locomotive, pulling one passenger car and 12 freight cars, entered the station. This train also carried munitions (presumably needed elsewhere more than in Vicksburg, which the train had just left) along with the household goods of two families who were fleeing the threatened river port.

By the time Colonel Grierson arrived on the scene with the rest of his force, the jubilant troopers of the lead battalion were already celebrating their exploit with a confiscated barrel of whiskey. Grierson quickly ordered them back to work destroying the military supplies, burning bridges, cutting down telegraph poles and ripping up track. A building full of Confederate uniforms and small arms was set afire, and the

89

two locomotives were blown up. At 2 p.m., Grierson's cavalrymen reassembled in the streets of Newton Station and galloped westward out of town.

General Pemberton was in Jackson, only 50 miles away. By now he knew that Grant had moved downriver and was posing some sort of threat. But Pemberton's attention was fixed on Benjamin Grierson, who had been roaming insolently through Mississippi all week long.

When word arrived of Grierson's presence in Newton Station, Pemberton reacted with everything he had. He sent two infantry regiments and a battery of artillery out from Jackson to block the raiders from the west. From the northern part of the state, he dispatched forces of cavalry and light artillery to block any movement by Grierson back toward Tennessee. He ordered General Franklin Gardner at Port Hudson to send all his "disposable cavalry" into southeastern Louisiana to cut off any escape in that direction. Pemberton already had another force of men in Meridian, to the east, assigned to hunt Grierson.

Pemberton was responding to the raid precisely as Grant had hoped. Grierson later estimated that at one time the Confederates had 20,000 men in the field hunting his raiders. And the scheduled Federal landing on the east bank of the Mississippi was just a few days away.

Meanwhile, Colonel Hatch's marauding Iowans and Captain Forbes's Company B were still on the loose, and just as the Confederates were trying to decide where Grierson would strike next, Forbes reentered the picture. Seeking to rejoin Grierson, he arrived at Newton Station 15 hours behind his commander and — believing a

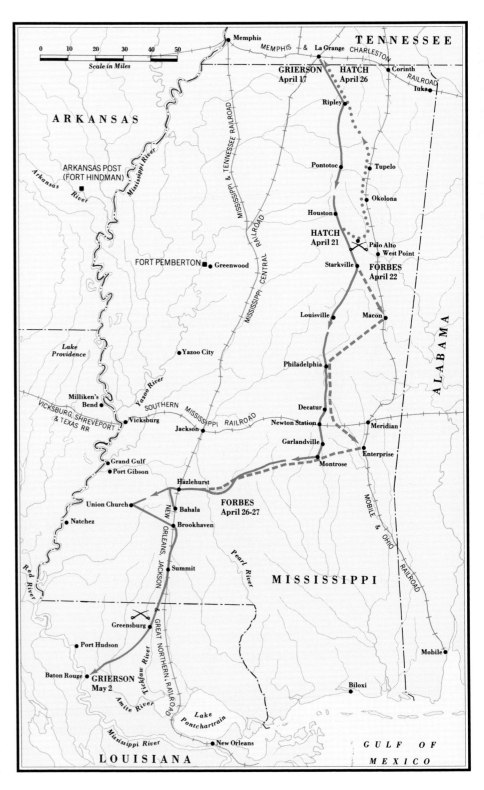

false report that Grierson had circulated before he left—headed east to catch up with the main column. In fact, Grierson had ridden westward.

The next day Forbes rode boldly into the town of Enterprise, Mississippi, southeast of Newton Station, having been told there were no Confederates there. In fact, the town was full of them. The resourceful Forbes instantly raised a white handkerchief, advanced on the stockade that was the Confederate headquarters, and in Grierson's name demanded the town's surrender.

The surprised Confederates asked for an hour to think it over. Forbes and his company fell back until they were safely out of sight, then turned and fled. "We never knew officially what the Confederates' reply was," Captain Forbes later wrote, "as for reasons best known to themselves they failed to make it reach us. Perhaps it was lack of speed. We fell back, very cheerfully, four miles, and fed, and resumed our retreat, which was diligently continued all night." The Confederates quickly sent word to Pemberton that Grierson's men had been seen east of Newton Station.

Grierson, meanwhile, pressed westward, having decided that instead of returning to La Grange, he would be most useful in support of General Grant's proposed landing at Grand Gulf.

As he made for the landing site, Grierson started to put the torch to bridges behind him to cut off Confederate pursuit, and Forbes's Company B was consequently in serious danger of being trapped. Forbes was now aware of Grierson's intention and was struggling desperately to catch up. On April 26, he chose three volunteers—one of them his brother Stephen, a sergeant—to ride

ahead on the company's freshest horses. "I never expected to see one of them again," Forbes later wrote.

That night, as the three riders galloped through the darkness, they saw lights ahead, then heard a shout in an unmistakably Northern accent: "Halt! Who goes there?" The three men spurred their horses. "Company B!" they cried.

There was a moment of astonished silence, and then the pickets yelled out, "Company B has come back!" The cheer was caught up by the rear company, Stephen Forbes recounted, and "it ran down the column, cheer upon cheer, faster than our horses could run." Sergeant Forbes pulled up beside Colonel Grierson, grinning. "Captain Forbes presents his compliments," he said, "and begs to be allowed to burn his bridges for himself."

The next day, April 27, Henry Forbes and Company B found a strong detachment that had been left by Grierson awaiting them at the nearest bridge; they burned it together and hurried on to rejoin Grierson at the Pearl River.

On the same day, the exhausted men of Colonel Hatch's regiment completed their mission, crossing back into Tennessee and regaining their base at La Grange.

By April 29, Grierson was only about 50 miles from Grand Gulf, but he was starting to worry. If Grant had landed, there should have been indications—fleeing civilians, troop movements or sounds of battle. So far there had been nothing.

Then, not far from Grand Gulf, Grierson encountered something that deeply concerned him. "The enemy," he wrote, "were now on our track in earnest. We were in the vicinity of their stronghold, and, from couri-

A Gallery of Western Cavalrymen

"War suits them," wrote Major General William Tecumseh Sherman in grudging admiration of the Confederate cavalrymen in the West. "The rascals are brave, fine riders, bold to rashness and dangerous in every sense."

In fact, the general could have paid equal tribute to the Federal cavalry assigned to the Vicksburg Campaign. Federal troopers from the frontier towns and farms of the West were natural horsemen, accustomed since boyhood to the

OHIO CORPORAL AND PRIVATE

CAPTAINS A. J. ALDEN AND J. M. ALDEN, BROTHERS IN THE 13TH ILLINOIS CAVALRY

PRIVATE J. M. SNIVELY, 7TH KANSAS CAVALRY

MICHIGAN CAVALRYMAN ARMED WITH A SPENCER REPEATING RIFLE

PRIVATE FRIEDRICH HOLDMANN, 2ND WISCONSIN CAVALRY

saddle. They were a match in every sense for their Southern rivals.

In the far-flung Western Theater, these rough and ready riders on both sides proved most effective as long-distance raiders, operating under enter-prising commanders such as the Con-federates' Nathan Bedford Forrest and the Federals' Benjamin Henry Grierson. Using surprise as a weapon, they struck hard at lines of communication, captur-ing or destroying anything in their path.

UNKNOWN PRIVATE, ALABAMA CAVALRY

UNKNOWN PRIVATE, TEXAS CAVALRY

PRIVATE ALEX SMITH, TENNESSEE CAVALRY

FROCK-COATED VOLUNTEER OF THE MISSISSIPPI CAVALRY

1ST MISSISSIPPI CAVALRYMAN

CONFEDERATE TROOPER FROM KENTUCKY

ers and dispatches which we captured, it was evident they were sending forces in all directions to intercept us." It was time to escape. From southwestern Mississippi there was only one refuge he could hope to reach: Baton Rouge, Louisiana, about 150 miles distant. That river port was now in Federal hands, and Grierson decided to head for it.

His men were approaching the limits of endurance. They had been covering 30 to 50 miles a day, sleeping little and eating what they could find in the countryside. As the troopers traveled, they replenished their stock of horses as best they could from farms and plantations. But even the freshest of their mounts — which now included mules — were flagging.

So far Grierson had managed to avoid any direct confrontation with Confederate forces. But on May 1, only a day's ride from Baton Rouge, he finally ran headlong into a fight. At a bridge over the Tickfaw River, an advance party of Grierson's troopers rode straight into three mounted companies of Confederates under Major James De Baun of the 9th Louisiana Partisan

Rangers. Almost immediately, five Federals were wounded and five captured. Moments later Grierson's main force thundered down the road, unlimbered an artillery piece, and drove De Baun's heavily outnumbered force back from the bridge.

Grierson moved his wounded into a nearby plantation house so that they would be sheltered from the elements until the Confederates found them. Then the cavalrymen mounted their horses and crossed the bridge, riding fast.

They dared not stop to rest that night, for Confederate forces were now swarming about them. The troopers were so tired that they nodded off as they rode; some had their legs tied together under their horses' bellies to keep from falling off. Captain Forbes and Company B were detailed to bring up the rear and collect stragglers, of which there were many. Forbes found sleeping soldiers riding as much as a mile behind their units. It often took a shaking of shoulders or a whack on the back to wake them.

At last, when the raiders were only six miles from Baton Rouge and Grierson con-

Grierson's cavalry charges onto a bridge across the Pearl River, east of Vicksburg, just in time to prevent the span from being destroyed by Confederate scouts (*right*) who are ripping up planks and throwing them into the river.

cluded that they were safely inside Federal lines, he stopped at a plantation house and allowed the men to fall out and rest. Grierson felt that he had to stay awake; the plantation house had a piano, and he sat down and played it.

Suddenly he was interrupted. One of his men rushed in and reported in some alarm that Confederate troops were approaching. Grierson knew better. "I rode out alone to meet the troops," he said, "without waking up my command."

Cautiously riding up the road were two companies of Union cavalry. As it happened, one of Grierson's sleeping riders had been carried by his horse into a Union encampment outside Baton Rouge; the troopers had been dispatched to check this man's incredible story that he was part of a Federal force that had just ridden through enemy territory all the way from Tennessee.

Grierson's arrival caused a sensation. Major General Christopher C. Augur, Federal commander in Baton Rouge, was awestruck by Grierson's achievement and insisted that his troopers must parade through the city. Grierson demurred, but Augur would not be refused. So the raiders were wakened and — ragged, caked with dust, and still half asleep — they staged a two-hour parade that afternoon through the streets of Baton Rouge, some of them dozing on their horses.

It had been an amazing exploit. "During the expedition," Grierson wrote in his report to Grant, "we killed and wounded about one hundred of the enemy, captured and paroled over 500 prisoners, many of them officers, destroyed between fifty and sixty miles of railroad and telegraph, captured and destroyed over 3,000 stand of arms, and other army stores and Government property to an immense amount; we also captured 1,000 horses and mules."

Grierson's raiders pause to burn a railroad station and tear up tracks at a depot in Mississippi. The raiders severed three key rail lines during their 600-mile foray.

Union losses, Grierson said, totaled 26 men killed, wounded, captured or missing. His troopers had come 600 miles in 16 days, and in the last day and a half they had covered an astonishing 76 miles, without stopping to eat or sleep.

Grant later described Grierson's Raid as "one of the most brilliant cavalry exploits of the war." Aside from statistical results, the venture had magnificently served its principal purpose, capturing the almost total attention of John Pemberton at a time when much more important events were occurring right on his doorstep.

During Grierson's Raid, Grant, poised on the west bank of the Mississippi, had come up with one more distraction for General Pemberton. North of Vicksburg, Sherman's corps was still positioned before the town's defenses. Somewhat tentatively, Grant suggested that these troops might make a feint against Vicksburg near Chickasaw Bluffs, the scene of Sherman's earlier, disastrous attack. "The effect of a heavy demonstration in that direction would be good as far as the enemy are concerned," Grant wrote Sherman, "but I am loath to order it, because it would be hard to make our own troops understand that only a demonstration was intended and our people at home would characterize it as a repulse. I therefore leave it to you whether to make such a demonstration."

Sherman, who prided himself on being a loyal subordinate, responded indignantly — and typically. "Does General Grant think I care what the newspapers say?" he asked a staff officer. He wrote to Grant: "We will make as strong a demonstration as possible. As to the reports in the newspapers, we

Captain Henry Forbes (*far left*) and his brother Stephen served together in Company B of Grierson's 7th Illinois Cavalry. Captain Forbes led his company of 35 horsemen on a dash eastward to cut the telegraph wires along the Mobile & Ohio Railroad.

must scorn them, else they will ruin us and our country."

He set off with 10 regiments on April 29, ordering the men to spread out over the decks of their transports so that they would "look as numerous as possible." Porter still had a few boats above Vicksburg, and they were ordered to get up steam so that the Confederates would think a major landing was planned. "The gunboats and transports whistled and puffed," said Captain William Jenney, Sherman's engineer officer, "and made all the noise they could. They showed themselves to the garrison and then drifted back and landed the men, who were marched through the woods until they were seen by the enemy." Then the soldiers were taken back on board the boats "to go through the same farce again."

Pemberton had dispatched reinforcements in the direction of Grand Gulf to help meet the threat from across the river, but now he received an alarming message from Brigadier General Carter L. Stevenson, his commander north of Vicksburg. "The demonstration at Grand Gulf must be only a

Spectators line the streets of Baton Rouge as Colonel Grierson leads his men into town on May 2, 1863. Although this illustration for *Harper's New Monthly Magazine* does not show it, the men were ragged and worn, their horses exhausted and lame from the ordeal.

feint," Stevenson telegraphed Pemberton in a panic. "Here is the real attack. The enemy are in front of me in force such as have never been seen before at Vicksburg. Send me reinforcements."

The regiments that had been sent to fight Grant were hastily ordered to turn around and head back to meet Sherman's thrust. Some of the Confederate soldiers were so exhausted by the time they got back to the town that citizens in carriages had to help them to their lines. They arrived just in time to see Sherman load his men into their transports for the last time and sail away.

Meanwhile, the naval bombardment of Grand Gulf had begun. Despite the fact that

Grant's various diversionary tactics had succeeded admirably, the Union fleet ran into stiff resistance.

Only two months before, Grand Gulf had been entirely undefended. Work on its gun emplacements had not been started until March 11, and by the time the Federals attacked on April 29 the defenses were still unfinished. Nevertheless, they were formidable — as Admiral Porter, who had the task of subduing them, quickly found out.

Situated near the junction of the Mississippi and Big Black Rivers, Grand Gulf was commanded by a promontory 50 feet high, and atop this bluff the Confederates had positioned 16 artillery pieces. Most of

A regiment of Illinois cavalry, possibly part of Grierson's newly arrived command, camps outside Baton Rouge in May 1863. Smoke rises from enlisted men's campfires in the background; the regimental headquarters tents in the foreground are shaded from the sun by an awning of boughs.

the cannon on board Porter's gunboats were far heavier than the Confederate pieces, and therefore the Union forces did not anticipate much trouble.

On the day of the assault, transports and barges loaded with the men of McClernand's XIII Corps stood out of range, ready to land. Some of the soldiers had been aboard those vessels for two days, and they soon discovered that they faced a longer wait.

As Grant watched from a tug in the middle of the Mississippi, the Federal fleet and the Confederate batteries pounded each other. The duel lasted five hours, and both sides did extensive damage. More than 2,500 Federal projectiles fell on the hilltop batteries, but the Confederates suffered only 18 casualties. Porter, down below, was hit much harder. He lost 18 killed and 56 wounded, and his vessels were battered — one of them, the *Tuscumbia,* so badly that it would be out of action for days. When the Federal gunboats renewed the attack three hours later, they were unable to silence the Confederate guns.

Grant went aboard Porter's flagship, the *Benton,* for a consultation. There seemed no point in hammering away any further at Grand Gulf. They must try to make a landing elsewhere. Grant still needed Grand Gulf as a supply port, but if he could get troops ashore farther to the south they could march back and take the town's fortifications from the rear. The soldiers were returned to the Louisiana bank and allowed to disembark, and Grant cast about for a new place to land.

Here as elsewhere along the Mississippi, the terrain was laced with waterways. A landing site would have to provide not only dry ground at the bank but also a dry route back to Grand Gulf. Only a local person

might know of such a place, and that evening soldiers abducted a slave from the east bank and brought him to headquarters. He pointed out a good landing spot: the village of Bruinsburg, eight miles downriver. It was high and dry.

The next day, April 30, McClernand's troops boarded their transports again and shortly thereafter were put ashore, unopposed, at Bruinsburg. The landing was anticlimactic, but Grant was jubilant. "I felt a

Admiral Porter's gunboats bombard Confederate artillery positions at Grand Gulf on April 29 to prepare for the crossing of Union troops below Vicksburg. Porter's fleet fired more than 2,500 rounds in five hours at the well-protected enemy guns.

the enemy. All the campaigns, labors, hardships and exposures that had been made and endured were for the accomplishment of this one object."

More men were on their way, but Grant did not wait. He knew that Confederate infantry at Grand Gulf would be coming to meet him, and he moved to strike first. The only route to Grand Gulf led inland, along the high ground through the little town of Port Gibson, 12 miles east of Bruinsburg and six miles southeast of Grand Gulf. McClernand's corps set out for Port Gibson that same afternoon.

The Confederate commander at Grand Gulf was 32-year-old Brigadier General John S. Bowen, a cool and highly regarded officer who had been a classmate of James B. McPherson's at West Point. Before the War, Bowen had been an architect in St. Louis, and a neighbor of Ulysses S. Grant's. Soon they would meet again, across the ridges and gullies of Port Gibson. Bowen would be at a distinct disadvantage. With some of his troops off chasing Benjamin Grierson, and several thousand more being held north of Vicksburg in response to Sherman's feint, Bowen had only 5,500 men to confront Grant's 20,000.

On April 30, Bowen, making the most of his meager resources, ordered Brigadier General Martin Green to place his brigade between Bruinsburg and Port Gibson in the expectation that the Union forces would come that way. Bowen held back most of his troops until he could be sure how the fighting was developing.

When night came and nothing had happened, Green rode forward to see where the Federals were. By a fork in the road he came upon the Shaifer house. The women who

degree of relief," he wrote, "scarcely ever equalled since." He was far from victorious, however, and did not minimize the remaining problems: "Vicksburg was not yet taken, it is true, nor were its defenders demoralized by any of our previous moves. I was now in the enemy's country, with a vast river and the stronghold of Vicksburg between me and my supplies." But Grant was a fighting man, and now at last he could fight. "I was on dry ground on the same side of the river with lived there were in near panic, hastily packing household goods in a wagon before taking refuge in Port Gibson. Green sought to calm them. There was plenty of time to pack, he said. The Yankees would not come before daylight. At that moment there was a rattle of gunfire. The women leaped into their wagon and fled, and Green hastily deployed his men to meet the attack.

But McClernand's troops were having second thoughts about pressing their attack. It was dark, and the ground was rough. For the remainder of the night there was only scattered fire. Both armies slept with their weapons and waited for daylight.

Grant later wrote that the terrain around Port Gibson was the most difficult he had ever seen: "The country in this part of Mississippi stands on edge, as it were, the roads running along the ridges except when they occasionally pass from one ridge to another. Where there are no clearings the sides of the hills are covered with a very heavy growth of timber and with undergrowth, and the ravines are filled with vines and canebrakes, almost impenetrable."

John Bowen made the best possible use of the rugged countryside. During the night his remaining troops began coming up, and he positioned them across the two ridgetop roads that ran from the direction of Bruinsburg into Port Gibson.

At 6 a.m., as McClernand's corps pushed forward from the vicinity of the Shaifer house, they divided forces; three divisions headed southeast on the Plantation Road, while the fourth division, under Brigadier General Peter J. Osterhaus, marched due east on the Bruinsburg Road. Because of the thick woods that lay between them, neither force could go to the aid of the other. Grant's

numerical advantage was not helping him much. It was the kind of country, said Grant, that made it "easy for an inferior force to delay, if not defeat, a far superior one." And sure enough, Bowen's four brigades, though greatly outnumbered, managed to keep both roads blocked. Sergeant T. B. Scott of the 6th Mississippi recalled that as the Federals deployed astride the Plantation Road, "we poured volley after volley into the crowded ranks of the infantry covering our entire front and right flank."

The Federals countered by bringing up their artillery and pounding the Confederate lines. The 1st Indiana Battery alone fired 1,050 rounds. Charles Willcox of the 33rd Illinois later evoked the scene: "Our artillery fires with powerful effect at them; we have now got a cross fire and an enfilading fire upon them. They have the woods; we have to go over an open field before our musketry can reach them, but there is a ridge upon which are our cannon, behind which we lie in almost perfect safety." Under the bombardment, the Confederate forces were almost helpless.

Bowen then sought to meet the threat. He stepped to the front of the 6th Mississippi and 23rd Alabama on the Confederate left, and crying "Follow me!" led them in a charge on a Federal artillery battery. Amid heavy fire, the Confederate soldiers went crashing through the brush behind their general, straight at the Union cannon. "We were able to drive the cannoneers out and take the guns," Captain W. C. Thompson of the 6th Mississippi recalled. But the Confederates now found themselves in an exposed position and were forced to abandon the guns and fall back. It had been a costly attack. "As we went back," the captain said, "we were amazed and shocked to see how many of our men were lying wounded in the path of our advance. We had paid heavily for those guns."

Around 11 a.m. on the Federal right, Brigadier General Alvin P. Hovey led the 34th Indiana and 56th Ohio in a charge on a battery of Virginia artillery 150 yards to his

In a healing gesture after the War, an Indiana volunteer named William Duffner presented this hand-crafted rocking chair to A. K. Shaifer, in whose yard the Battle of Port Gibson had begun. A map painted on the seat traces the 24th Indiana's advance through Mississippi, and on the back is a picture of Shaifer's house. The inscription reads in part: "May God forgive, unite and bless us all."

front. The Federals gave a cheer and started forward with fixed bayonets, but they did not get far. Raked by canister and musket fire, many of Hovey's men halted and began to take cover.

Seeing them waver, Hovey rode up and rallied his troops. "Again the bright bayonets were glittering in the sun," he remembered, "again a wild shout, a shout of triumph, reverberated through the hills." Ahead, two companies of the 11th Indiana flanked the Confederate battery and began shooting down the gunners and their horses. The blueclad ranks swept over the battery, capturing two guns, the flag of the 15th Arkansas and 220 prisoners.

The Federal breakthrough spurred General Bowen into desperate action. The Confederate commander led the 3rd and 5th Missouri in a counterattack that plugged the hole in his line, and even threatened for a moment to turn the Federal right. But fresh Federal troops then entered the battle. Confederate ammunition was running low, and as the afternoon wore on Bowen realized his position was hopeless. Three miles to the north, the standoff on the Bruinsburg Road had finally been broken by Grant, who had sent part of McPherson's XVII Corps to bolster Osterhaus' division. McPherson's troops, charging through brush and canebrake, managed to flank the smaller Confederate force. By late in the day the Confederates were retreating along both roads, although still in good order. When night fell, the Union forces held the field; Grant's advance elements were within two miles of the town.

The following morning Bowen was gone. He had fought magnificently against enormous odds, delaying the Union advance and

inflicting 875 casualties. With substantial re-inforcements he might have turned the battle around. But his small force had paid a stiff price, losing 832 men killed, wounded or captured. Among the dead was a brigadier general, Edward D. Tracy. And as the Federals mopped up during the next few days, another 1,000 Confederate soldiers were captured. Bowen had lost more than one third of his command.

He was soon compelled to give up more than Port Gibson. Grand Gulf was now untenable, and on the night of May 7 he withdrew all forces from that bastion, leaving behind five large guns in his haste.

Grant's beachhead was now secure. Grant ordered McClernand to pursue the retreating Confederates, and instructed his rear echelons — including Sherman's corps — to move up at the double. He then went aboard his headquarters steamer and took a bath (he had not been out of his clothes in a week) and took some time to deal with an array of visitors who had turned up.

One of them was the general's son Fred, who was having an adventurous time. Without his father's knowledge, the youngster had talked his way onto one of the transports included in the second group to run the Vicksburg batteries — the group from which

Retained by the War Department to keep an eye on Grant, the distinguished former editor Charles A. Dana became the general's eloquent advocate in his reports to Lincoln and Secretary of War Stanton. Grant, Dana wrote, was "not an original or brilliant man, but sincere, thoughtful, deep and gifted with courage that never faltered."

the three reporters had been captured. Once aboard, Fred refused to go below; instead, he crouched on deck behind a coil of cable and watched the spectacle while shells burst all around him. He soon rejoined his father and landed with him at Bruinsburg. Grant then left the boy sleeping on a gunboat there — hoping, he said, "to get away without him until after Grand Gulf should fall into our hands."

But Fred caught up with his father again near Port Gibson, arriving in the company of another of Grant's visitors, Charles A. Dana, the former managing editor of the New York *Tribune*, and now a special representative of Secretary of War Stanton. The two had started for Port Gibson on foot, but on the way a Union officer had made them a gift of a couple of captured plow horses. "The first time I call to mind seeing either of them after the battle," wrote Grant with evident amusement, "they were mounted on two enormous horses, grown white from age, each equipped with dilapidated saddles and bridles." (Fred's bridle was, in fact, a piece of clothesline.)

Dana's role in Grant's entourage was a curious one. He had shown up at Milliken's Bend a few weeks before, and had instantly been recognized by Grant's staff as a spy sent by the Secretary of War to check out the increasingly hostile press accounts of Grant — stories that portrayed the general as drunken and inept. Stanton had sent others on this mission as well, including Inspector General Lorenzo Thomas, who was at the moment the guest of Admiral Porter on a gunboat in the river.

Some of Grant's staff had been angry about Dana's assignment, and there had even been talk of throwing him in the river, but wiser heads had prevailed. Dana was welcomed; all his questions were answered; he was given free access to information, invited to dine at Grant's mess and treated like one of the family.

Dana responded favorably. He soon discerned Grant's qualities as a commander, and communicated his findings at length to Stanton. Lincoln was shown the messages, but he did not really need much reassurance. "I think we'll try him a little longer," he had said when critics urged Grant's removal. "He fights."

Grant was pleased to have Dana around. He liked the man. Moreover, as long as the former editor was sending long reports to Stanton, Grant felt no obligation to do so. Dana's presence thus relieved him of a substantial burden of paper work.

Another visitor, Governor Richard Yates of Illinois, who was also reported to be a Stanton spy, was sticking close to the headquarters of his fellow Illinois politician, John McClernand. Both men had been delighted by the showing of McClernand's Illinois soldiers at Port Gibson. Those soldiers were of course voters as well, and when Yates and McClernand encountered them in the field one day they could not resist pausing to make a few remarks.

Grant, waiting nearby, watched the speechmaking for a while, then mildly suggested to the two that it might be time to get back to the War. Grant had little patience with self-promotion, and he knew well that the campaign was far from over. A foothold had been gained, but now his army must push northward to Vicksburg, where his leadership again would face the test of fire.

This photograph of Grant was taken in the early 1850s before he resigned his captain's commission to avoid a court-martial for drinking and neglecting his duty. At the time, he was stationed on the West Coast, apart from his wife and family.

Grant (*left*) and his friend Alexander Hays, both second lieutenants, stand beside their horses at Camp Salubrity, Louisiana, in 1845. Hays later became a general and was killed fighting under Grant in 1864.

Grant was a 27-year-old quartermaster of the 4th U.S. Infantry at Sackets Harbor, New York, when this daguerreotype was taken in 1849. Recently married, he lived with his bride, Julia, in cramped quarters at Madison Barracks.

The Union's Homespun Hero

Exalted in the eyes of the Northern public, Major General Ulysses S. Grant was in person a shy and reticent man, as plain as homespun. "He was pictured in the popular mind as striding about in the swash-buckler style of melodrama," a Federal officer wrote. "Many of us were not a little surprised to find in him a modesty of mien and gentleness of manner which seemed to fit him more for the court than for the camp."

Approaching the apex of his military career in 1863, Major General Grant poses with his hand on his sword. In fact, he disliked side arms and wore them only rarely.

This portrait of Grant was taken in Vicksburg after his victory there in 1863. "His eyes were dark grey, and were the most expressive of his features,'" an aide wrote. "His face gave little indication of his thoughts."

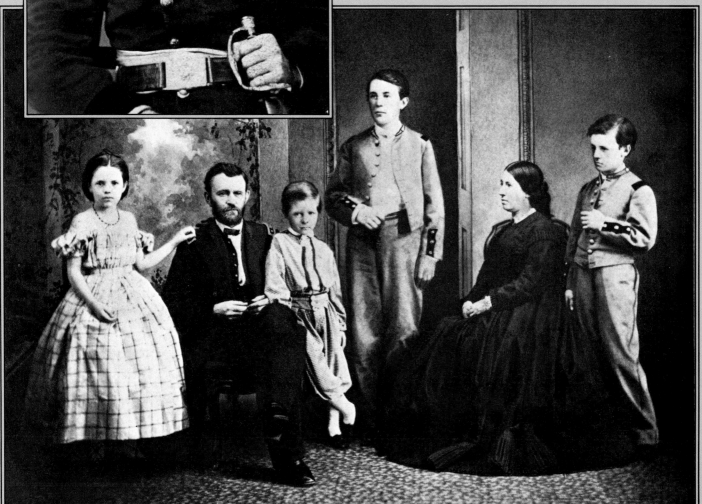

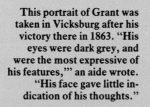

Toward the end of the War, Grant and his wife, Julia, sit for a family portrait with their children (*from left*), Nellie, Jesse, Fred and Ulysses Jr.

The Sweep to the Big Black

Now that he was safely across the Mississippi and consolidating his position around Grand Gulf, Grant made plans to send one of his corps downriver to help General Nathaniel Banks take Port Hudson. Once that Confederate strongpoint fell, Grant could establish a supply line running north from New Orleans. Then Banks and Grant together would tackle Vicksburg.

This approach had the approval not only of General Halleck, but of President Lincoln himself. But Grant had no sooner entered Grand Gulf than he received a message from Banks, dispatched from deep inside Louisiana. Although Banks was aware of the cooperative plan, he had suddenly embarked on an independent campaign along waterways west of the Mississippi *(page 110)*. Banks wrote that it would be May 10 before he could attack Port Hudson. Vicksburg would have to come after that, and Banks would be able to spare only 15,000 men — far fewer than Grant had anticipated — to help in the assault.

This put a different face on things. "To wait for his cooperation would have detained me at least a month," Grant wrote later. "The reinforcements would not have reached 10,000 men after deducting casualties and necessary river guards." And meanwhile the Confederates, now off balance, would have a chance to recover, concentrate their forces and undo everything Grant had achieved with his successful crossing.

There was another consideration, one that

Grant did not mention but that must have been on his mind. Banks was Grant's senior in rank; in a joint operation the Massachusetts politician would be the superior officer.

In any case, Grant concluded that he could not wait. He wrote later, "I therefore determined to move independently of Banks, cut loose from my base, destroy the rebel force in the rear of Vicksburg and invest or capture the city."

Grant dutifully wrote out a dispatch notifying Halleck of the change in plans, even though he knew well that, as he put it later, "Halleck's caution would lead him to disapprove." Grant was, after all, committing himself against an enemy that would substantially outnumber him if Pemberton and Johnston could unite their forces. But communications with Washington were very difficult at the moment; the nearest Federal telegraph station was at Cairo, Illinois, more than 400 miles away. Indeed, Grant was counting on that. The time it would take to reach Washington and get a reply would be so great, Grant wrote, "that I could not be interfered with until it was demonstrated whether my plan was practicable."

Success would hinge on adequate sources of supply. Since the landing, Grant had been collecting all the vehicles he could find on nearby plantations. The resulting supply train was a hodgepodge of farm wagons, fine carriages, surreys, buckboards, buggies and carts, drawn by assorted horses, mules and oxen. When Sherman, last of the corps

Private Gustavus Martin of the 45th Illinois displays his tin coffee cup and a piece of hardtack. Late in the Vicksburg Campaign, food was so short that Federal soldiers subsisted on coffee, hardtack and whatever else they could scavenge from the countryside.

commanders to cross the river, found this wild collection of vehicles clogging the road from Grand Gulf, he foresaw chaos, and sent a warning to Grant: "This road will be jammed as sure as life if you attempt to supply 50,000 men by one single road."

Grant's reply outlined his unorthodox strategy: "I do not calculate upon the possibility of supplying the army with full rations from Grand Gulf. I know it will be impossible without constructing additional roads. What I do expect, however, is to get up what rations of hard bread, coffee and salt we can, and make the country furnish the balance."

Life for the troops was going to be difficult, but they were already used to living off the land. The troops were proving such able foragers that Fred Grant often ate with the enlisted men rather than at his father's mess because the food was better. Many soldiers, however, lacked blankets and tents, and one brigadier reported that nearly a third of his men were marching barefoot.

Grant willingly shared the hardships of his men. Charles Dana wrote that the night after the crossing, Grant had slept on the ground, "without a tent, in the midst of his soldiers, with his saddle for a pillow and without even an overcoat for covering." And after Grand Gulf was secured, Dana noted, Grant slept "upon a hard wooden bench, this time without even the luxury of a saddle."

Pemberton, in his Vicksburg headquarters, was probably not sleeping as well as Grant. As soon as the Confederate commander had fathomed Grant's intentions, he had sent a call for help to General Joseph Johnston at Tullahoma, Tennessee. Johnston — still ailing from the severe wound he had received at the Battle of Seven Pines outside Richmond

almost a year before — could spare Pemberton no troops, but he offered some excellent advice: "If Grant's army lands on this side of the river, the safety of Mississippi depends on beating it. For that object you should unite your whole force." He repeated his counsel the next day; and then, knowing that Pemberton's reluctance to leave Vicksburg undefended in order to pursue Grant reflected the cautious policy of President Davis, Johnston added: "Success will give you back what was abandoned to win it."

Grant was already taking steps to prevent such a concentration of forces against him. He started his army on a forced march northward to get between the defenders of Vicksburg and the Confederates at Jackson; two brigades were already there, and two more had been sent by General Johnston. Grant intended to destroy the force at Jackson, then wreck the rail hub through which any Confederate reinforcements must pass.

Grant's scouts reported that Pemberton's troops were digging entrenchments west of the Big Black River, which Grant would have to cross to get at Vicksburg. Evidently, Pemberton expected Grant to head straight for the city, and Grant made a diversion in that direction to keep him thinking that way. When Sherman's XV Corps embarked at Milliken's Bend to join the army at Grand Gulf, the transports detoured up the Yazoo and the troops faked a landing at Haynes' Bluff. The vessels soon steamed back down the river to Grand Gulf. Confused by the feint, Pemberton could not decide whether to heed Davis' counsel to stay in Vicksburg or Johnston's advice to come out and fight. Trying to do both, he moved cautiously out of the town with about 20,000 troops, but he left roughly 10,000 men behind. He concen-

Clearing the Bayou Teche

In April 1863, Major General Nathaniel Banks launched a campaign in Louisiana to secure the west bank of the Mississippi and thus isolate the Confederate bastion of Port Hudson on the east bank. Banks hoped to cut off enemy supplies from this fertile region and destroy the 4,000-man force of Major General Richard Taylor, encamped on Bayou Teche west of New Orleans.

Banks's plan was to catch the Confederates in a pincers movement. While 10,000 Federals led by Brigadier Generals William Emory and Godfrey Weitzel moved up the Teche, Brigadier General Cuvier Grover was to lead 5,000 men up the Atchafalaya River on a roughly parallel route, land at a place called Indian Bend (*below*), and hit the Confederates from the rear.

Sensing the trap, Taylor withdrew his force to Fort Bisland, a formidable earthworks near the mouth of the Teche. There on April 12 and 13, his men beat back several attacks by Emory and Weitzel, then slipped away upstream. On the 14th, at a bow in the Teche called Irish Bend, they met Grover's Federals. After a sharp fight, the Confederates escaped again and headed up the Teche to its junction with the Red River.

Although Taylor had eluded Banks, the Teche was now in Federal hands, along with huge quantities of enemy supplies. More important, the Port Hudson garrison could no longer count on help from across the Mississippi.

From transports in the Atchafalaya River, Federal troops storm ashore at Indian Bend, forcing a small detachment of Confederates to withdraw. Aboard the steamers, a Federal wrote, "we were packed closer than sardines in a box. So close that we didn't have room to sweat."

trated his forces near the railroad town of Edwards Depot, 13 miles east of the port city, and there he waited for Grant's attack.

Meanwhile, he had ordered up from Port Hudson a brigade of 2,500 men commanded by Brigadier General John Gregg. As instructed, Gregg's force moved up through Jackson and then marched west for about 15 miles to the town of Raymond. Pemberton warned Gregg to look for a Federal feint in his direction, but predicted that Grant's main attack would come at the Big Black River. Thus Gregg would be in a perfect position to strike Grant's flank and rear.

Pemberton had failed to make even elementary arrangements for scouting the Federal movements, and so did not know that Grant was marching hard not for the Big Black and Vicksburg but for Jackson. McPherson's 10,000-man XVII Corps was in the lead, and Gregg's understrength brigade was directly in its path. Early on the morning of May 12 they made contact. Gregg had been ordered to fall back to Jackson if he encountered a superior force. But he assumed that McPherson's vanguard was a smaller unit making the feint he had been told to expect. So, at noon, Gregg attacked.

The opposing forces were separated by a sluggish stream, called Fourteen-Mile Creek, that ran roughly east-west. Gregg sent two of his regiments, the 7th Texas and 3rd Tennessee, south across the creek to pin down the approaching Federals, while four regiments were dispatched to ford the creek to the east and hit McPherson's right flank.

Gregg's tactics worked well at first, despite the Federals' numerical superiority. McPherson's lead brigade was unable to maintain its formation in the tangled woods lining the creek bank and was soon halted by fire from the concealed Confederates. As more Federal troops came up, the Texans and Tennesseans launched a furious attack, slamming into the 23rd Indiana. In the thick woods, the lines of battle soon became disorganized. Neither side was able to fix bayonets, the Confederates because they had none and the Indianians because there was not enough time. After a brief melee with clubbed muskets and fists, the Federals broke for the rear, pursued by the Confederates. Panic spread rapidly among the Federals, and for a few minutes it seemed as if their entire line would crumble. Then Major General John A. Logan, commander of McPherson's 3rd Division, appeared on the scene.

Logan was a 36-year-old former attorney and Congressman from Illinois who had proved during two years of war to be an exception to the rule that political appointees made poor soldiers. Though not a tall man, Logan was an impressive figure, sharp-featured and powerfully built, with a booming, orator's voice. His swarthy complexion, shoulder-length black hair and sweeping mustache had earned him the nickname "Black Jack," and his troops regarded him with awe. Logan spurred his black horse into the midst of his wavering line, and with what one soldier called "the shriek of an eagle" rallied the men and launched a counterattack. The outnumbered Confederates resisted fiercely, but step by step were driven back across the creek. In the dense growth along the bank, the enemy ranks were so close to each other for a time, said Colonel Manning Force of the 20th Ohio, that the "rifles of opposing lines crossed while firing." Many of the wounded suffered powder burns from weapons fired at point-blank range.

By the time Gregg's regiments to the east

Staff officers of the U.S. Army's XVII Corps assemble for a portrait around their commander, Major General James B. McPherson (*seated, second from right*). The 34-year-old McPherson, born in a log cabin in Ohio, graduated first in his class at West Point and later earned Grant's trust as his engineer officer at Shiloh.

launched their flank attack, Logan's Federals were in command along the creek. Still, Gregg would not recall his men. "At them we went," reported Lieutenant Colonel James Turner of the 30th Tennessee, "yelling like savages." Their courage was to no avail. Decimated by volleys in front and flank, the Confederates faltered, then fell back. By 2 p.m. Gregg's brigade was retreating toward Raymond, pursued by the Federals.

It was a costly little victory. The Federals had lost 442 men. The Confederates' toll was 514, with the 7th Texas and 3rd Tennessee accounting for 345 of those casualties.

That afternoon the discouraged Gregg, aware at last of the size of McPherson's force,

abandoned Raymond and headed for Jackson. The day before, when Gregg had arrived in Raymond, the anxious townspeople had welcomed his men as saviors, and they had been preparing a great picnic for the brigade when the battle started. The hot, hungry Union soldiers found the feast waiting there as they entered the town on Gregg's heels, and they wolfed down the food before continuing the pursuit toward Jackson.

The residents of Jackson, meanwhile, were about to welcome a distinguished visitor, General Joseph E. Johnston. Four days earlier, as he lay ailing in Tennessee, he had received a telegram from the Confederate Sec-

retary of War. The message instructed him to start at once for Mississippi to "take chief command of the forces, giving to those in the field, as far as practicable, the encouragement and benefit of your personal direction." Johnston wired back: "I shall go immediately, although unfit for service." And the next morning, accompanied by his physician, he boarded a train for Jackson. Jackson was only about 300 miles away, but the Federals threatened all the direct routes; Johnston had to go through Atlanta, Montgomery and Mobile, roughly doubling the distance. Exhausted, he reached Jackson on May 13, the day after the Battle of Raymond.

Johnston found himself in the backwash of defeat. Gregg's weary men were straggling into town; Federals were on the outskirts. Pemberton was at Edwards Depot, cut off from Jackson by Union forces so that Johnston had great difficulty communicating with him. More troops were coming in from Port Hudson, as well as from Tennessee and South Carolina, and Johnston would soon have 12,000 men in Jackson. But Grant was approaching with at least 20,000 troops, and Johnston, still sick, was too dispirited to risk another defeat. In a dispatch to Richmond, he revealed his dismay: "I am too late."

The next morning, in a drenching rain, Johnston began to withdraw to the north. His scouts reported the approach of two Federal corps, Sherman's from the southwest and McPherson's from the town of Clinton, eight miles west of Jackson. Johnston left behind General Gregg, with two brigades and a regiment of mounted infantry, to cover his retreat. Gregg stationed the brigades of Brigadier General W.H.T. Walker and Colonel Peyton H. Colquitt astride the Clinton road and assigned the 3rd Kentucky Mounted Infantry and a handful of sharpshooters to guard the southwest approach.

Around noon McPherson's soldiers, slogging along in the rain on a road covered by a foot of water, came up against Walker's and Colquitt's brigades. McPherson had trouble getting into position; his artillery sank into the mud, and Confederate cannon fire cut down many in his ranks. Then, just as McPherson was ready to attack, the rain started to come down so hard that he was forced to delay, fearing that his troops' cartridge powder would be too wet to fire.

The Confederates used the time to throw up entrenchments on the outskirts of Jackson, and when at last McPherson's men got under way, they found themselves fighting a determined foe in a formidable position. For a while they made little progress. But the Federals greatly outnumbered the Confederates, and the division commander leading the attack, Brigadier General Marcellus M. Crocker, grew impatient at the standoff. Calling up the four regiments of Colonel Samuel A. Holmes's brigade, he sent them forward in a bayonet charge. Although under heavy fire, the troops advanced "at double quick, cheering wildly," recalled Major Francis Deimling of the Union's 19th Missouri. For a few minutes the Confederates bravely stood their ground, the 24th South Carolina grappling hand to hand with the

10th Missouri, but the Federal advance was relentless. At last, the defenders gave way.

To the south, Sherman's men had little trouble brushing aside the Kentucky infantrymen. Colonel L. F. Hubbard reported that his 5th Minnesota swept into Jackson "with bayonets fixed and with exultant shouts." Soon men of the 59th Indiana were flying their flag from the dome of the state capitol. As the Federals pressed on into the city, Captain Samuel Byers of the 5th Iowa paused for a moment. "I noticed a man in a field quite alone, digging in the ground," he said. "Out of curiosity I went to him and asked what he was doing alone when the regiments were all hurrying away. A brown blan-

ket covered something nearby. He pointed to it and said that two of his brothers lay dead under that blanket. He was digging a grave for them. He went on with his work and I hurried to overtake my command."

For a rearguard action, the Battle of Jackson had been surprisingly bloody. Federal losses totaled 300, while Gregg's Confederates had lost 200 men, most of them from Colquitt's brigade.

The departure of Gregg's troops from Jackson had been so precipitate that some residents were not even aware of it until Federal soldiers suddenly appeared. The streets and hotel corridors were filled with convalescent Confederates and, according to one report, with deserters. Moreover, someone had opened the doors of the state prison, and in all the confusion inmates joined Federal soldiers in an orgy of looting.

Jackson was a manufacturing town, prized by the Federals less for what they could extract from it themselves than for what they could deny the Confederates. At Grant's order, large parts of the city were put to the torch. "Foundries, machine shops, warehouses, factories, arsenals and public stores were fired as fast as flames could be kindled," reported the Northern journalist Sylvanus Cadwallader. More important, both of the rail lines passing through Jackson were destroyed. Sherman's soldiers tore up the tracks, started fires with the ties and then, to ensure that the rails would never be used again, heated them over the flames until they were soft enough to be twisted around trees.

That night Grant slept in the same hotel room that Johnston had used just the night before. But Grant had no intention of remaining in the Mississippi capital. It was time to strike at his real target.

In this endeavor, he now had a stroke of luck: He got a look at Johnston's plans.

Behind this good fortune lay a fascinating tale. Some time before, a Memphis citizen had been exiled from that city with much publicity by General Stephen A. Hurlbut, Grant's commander there. Hurlbut had publicly labeled the man disloyal to the Union and ordered him not to come back. But the expulsion had been staged; the miscreant was in fact a Federal spy, who had quickly obtained a job as a Confederate courier. As fate would have it, he had been selected by Johnston to carry a message to Pemberton. The spy had brought the message to McPherson, who now showed it to Grant.

"I have lately arrived," Johnston's note read, "and learn that Major General Sherman is between us with four divisions at Clinton. It is important to re-establish communication, that you may be reinforced. If practicable, come up in his rear at once. To beat such a detachment would be of immense value. The troops here could cooperate. All the strength you can quickly assemble should be brought; time is all-important."

Johnston was mistaken about Sherman's position, but now that Grant knew what both Confederate generals were going to do, he was perfectly willing to send them some forces to fight. Confident that a command of sufficient size, aggressively led, could smash the Confederates when they tried to spring their trap, Grant had the letter resealed and sent on its way. Then he issued immediate orders to General McClernand, who was south of the rail line between Jackson and Vicksburg, to move north and place his XIII Corps between the two Confederate forces. McPherson marched out of Jackson with his corps the next day to support McClernand.

On the outskirts of Jackson, troops of the 17th Iowa, 80th Ohio and 10th Missouri charge across open ground into the concentrated fire of Colonel Peyton H. Colquitt's South Carolinians on May 14, 1863. At a cost of 200 casualties, the Federals drove the Confederates from their protected position and swept on into the Mississippi capital.

Pemberton, meanwhile, was in a quandary back at Edwards Depot. If he did as Johnston urged, he would leave Vicksburg uncovered, thus violating both Jefferson Davis' directives and his own inclinations. He delayed acting, and late on May 14 called a council of war—the first he had ever convened—and asked his generals which course they preferred. After a vigorous discussion, a majority favored Johnston's plan, but several preferred a third option—to head south and cut Grant's supply line. To be sure, that too would leave Vicksburg unprotected; nevertheless, Pemberton judged "the only possibility of success to be in the plan of cutting the enemy's communications." They were all unaware, of course, that Grant was fully prepared to continue the campaign even if his supply line was cut.

And then Pemberton, having dispatched troops south toward Raymond, was shaken from his decision. He received another, more urgent message from Johnston, who was still north of Jackson, calling once again for Pemberton to move toward him. This time Pemberton decided to follow orders. He instructed the troops that were already marching south to turn northward and rendezvous with Johnston's force at the town of Clinton. They were about halfway there when the Federals intercepted them, at a hill on the farm of a man named Sid Champion.

Pemberton had 23,000 men at Champion's Hill to face the 32,000 Federals of McClernand's and McPherson's corps. Sherman's corps was en route from Jackson, and Grant had galloped ahead to take command of the battle. Although the Confederate defense had to be hastily improvised, the terrain Pemberton selected could scarcely have been better. He deployed his three divisions a mile east of meandering Baker's Creek to cover the bridges on the Jackson and the Raymond roads (*map, page 118*). His line, taking the shape of a fishhook, extended from the Raymond road four miles northeast to the crest of Champion's Hill, then curved back two miles west to where the Jackson road crossed Baker's Creek. Major General Carter L. Stevenson commanded Pemberton's left, Major General John S. Bowen the center, and Major General William W. Loring the right. Champion's Hill was the key to the position. It was, Grant remembered, "one of the highest points in that section, and commanded all the ground in range."

The battle began in the south, where Major General Andrew Jackson Smith's Federal division, marching west on the Raymond road, came under the fire of Loring's artillery. Both sides deployed skirmishers, and a hot fight ensued. But the bloodiest encounter would be to the north. Grant intended the bulk of McClernand's XIII Corps to strike the angle of Pemberton's line at Champion's Hill from the east, while Logan's division of McPherson's corps attacked from the north. As usual, McClernand displayed little initiative, and only one of his divisions came into action. Fortunately for the Federals, this division was commanded by the ambitious and combative Brigadier General Alvin P. Hovey, who had fought so hard at Port Gibson.

At 10:30 a.m., hearing the opening volleys of Logan's troops to his right, Hovey sent his two brigades in a headlong charge up Champion's Hill. Holding the Confederate left, General Stevenson's line was stretched so thin at this point that some regiments were separated by as much as 300 yards. Taken by surprise, the Confederates gave way.

Confederate guards relax outside the remains of a covered bridge, converted into a prison for captive Federals.

A Prison over the Pearl

When Federal troops took Jackson, Mississippi, on May 14, 1863, they liberated fellow soldiers held captive in an unusual Confederate prison — the ruin of a covered bridge on the Pearl River.

One of the prisoners was Colonel Thomas Clement Fletcher, who drew the sketch above in pencil on ruled paper — the only materials available. Colonel Fletcher, commander of the 31st Missouri "Wide Awake" Zouaves, had been wounded and captured the previous December during General Sherman's ill-fated offensive at Chickasaw Bluffs.

Conditions for Fletcher, and for the 19 other officers and 380 enlisted men crowded within the rickety structure, were miserable. During the winter of 1862-1863, the prisoners had to endure the cold without benefit of beds or blankets. Afraid that the bridge might burn, the Confederates allowed no fires, or even candles, inside. Exposure and disease caused frequent deaths among the inmates. Almost every day, according to an account published in *Harper's Weekly*, "two or three were carried out dead, and sometimes the dead lay at the entrance of the bridge unburied for four days."

Fletcher was one of the lucky inmates; he survived the ordeal, and in 1865 became the first postwar governor of Missouri.

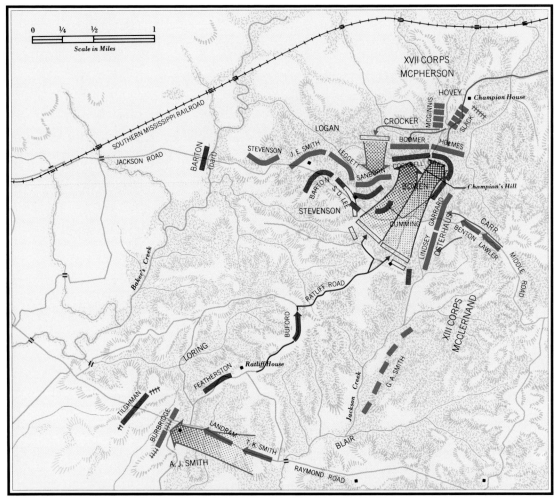

On the morning of May 16, Alvin Hovey's Federals seized Champion's Hill, only to be repulsed about 1:30 p.m. by John Bowen's Confederate division. When William Loring's division failed to advance in support of Bowen, Federal reinforcements from John Logan's and Marcellus Crocker's divisions were able to move into the breach. By late afternoon the Confederates were in full retreat southwestward toward the lower bridge over Baker's Creek.

Driving the enemy before them, General George F. McGinnis' Federal brigade crested the hill and came face to face with half a dozen Confederate artillery batteries. Just before the guns spewed out their lethal charges of canister, McGinnis ordered his regiments to fall prone. The iron balls whistled harmlessly overhead, and before many of the Confederate gunners could reload or limber up, the blue ranks were upon them. Captain Samuel J. Ridley's Mississippi Battery managed to get off a last round of double-shotted canister that tore scores of Federals to pieces, but the 11th Indiana wad-ed into the Confederates with bayonets and rifle butts, and captured the guns. Ridley fell with six wounds, and later died.

By 1 p.m. the Confederate left was crumbling. Realizing that his army faced disaster, Pemberton issued a frantic call for reinforcements from Bowen's and Loring's divisions to the south. Both generals refused to respond, protesting that there were masses of Federal troops to their front. Pemberton repeated his orders, and at 1:30 Bowen marched toward the sound of the guns. Incredibly, Loring again refused to move.

Bowen then launched a counterattack

against Hovey's troops on Champion's Hill, with Colonel Francis M. Cockrell's Missouri brigade on the left and Brigadier General Martin Green's Arkansas brigade on the right. Screaming the Rebel yell, Bowen's men struck with what one Federal called "terrific fierceness," and soon it was Hovey's bluecoats who were falling back. When the 24th Indiana began to break, Lieutenant Colonel R. F. Barter seized his regimental colors to rally the men, only to go down badly wounded by a volley that riddled the flag and shattered its staff. In minutes, 201 of the 500 men in the 24th Indiana fell. Hovey reported that his division retreated "slowly and stubbornly, contesting with death every inch of the field they had won." One Federal remembered the sight of a staff officer carrying an order forward in the face of roaring musket fire, one hand held up over his eyes as if to protect them from a driving rain.

Grant, meanwhile, ordered the nearest troops at hand—two brigades from XVII Corps under Colonels George Boomer and Samuel Holmes—to rush to Hovey's aid. Private M. O. Frost of the Union's 10th Missouri recalled what happened when the orders came: "Although we had traveled 12 miles under the hot sun we started on the run; knapsacks, haversacks, blankets and everything except our guns and cartridge boxes were thrown to the side of the road. We started up the hill with yells and shouts that made the earth tremble." As the 5th Iowa moved up, Captain Byers saw scores of wounded men—"almost whole companies"—streaming down off the hill. The men did not seem demoralized, Byers recalled. "Some of them were laughing, and yelling at us: 'Wade in and give them hell!'"

As Byers approached the summit with the Federal reinforcements, he saw "a solid wall of men in gray, their muskets at their shoulders blazing in our faces and their batteries of artillery roaring as if it were the end of the world. For over an hour we loaded our guns and killed each other as fast as we could."

Sergeant Charles Longley of the 24th Iowa marveled that in the thick of battle a kind of madness gripped the men: "Every human instinct is carried away by a torrent of passion, kill, kill, KILL, seems to fill your heart and be written over the face of all nature." Soldiers on both sides fired the 40 rounds in their cartridge boxes and then scrabbled among the dead for more.

On the Federal right flank atop Champion's Hill, the men of the 34th Indiana were in their first big fight. Some of the soldiers, badly shaken, were starting for the rear when General Logan appeared on the field with what one soldier called "the speed of a cyclone." Sergeant J. B. Harris watched Logan rein up in front of the outfit, shouting that "he had been wounded five times and never turned his back to the foe yet." The general "spoke no parables," Harris recalled. "His language was forcible, inspiring, and savored a little of brimstone." When the adjutant of the 34th protested that "the Rebels are awful thick up there," Logan roared, "Damn it, that's the place to kill them— where they are thick!" The men of the 34th rallied, and Logan led them forward.

Around 2:30 p.m. McClernand finally bestirred himself and ordered Brigadier General Peter J. Osterhaus' division forward. Hovey had driven Pemberton's left back until the Confederate line faced almost due north; now Osterhaus' advance from the east threatened Bowen's right flank. It was crucial that Loring's division come into action.

But it was only after Pemberton personally delivered the order to his recalcitrant subordinate that Loring got moving.

By then it was too late. The defense of Champion's Hill had collapsed, and the men, as one of Loring's officers put it, were "rushing pell-mell from the scene of action." A colonel who tried to stem the panic reported: "I brought my regiment to the charge bayonets, but even this could not check them in their flight. The colors of three regiments passed through. We collared them, begged them and abused them in vain."

Realizing that all was lost, Pemberton issued orders for a general retreat. But Logan's Federals had cut the Jackson road, and the only route of escape across Baker's Creek was the Raymond road bridge on Pemberton's southern flank. Pemberton ordered Brigadier General Lloyd Tilghman to hold his position one mile east of the crossing "at all hazards." Had the Federals facing Tilghman's brigade launched an attack, the Confederate army might well have been destroyed. As it was, the battle sputtered out in an artillery duel. One of the last casualties was the brave Tilghman. He had dismounted beside a battery and was sighting one of the guns when a Federal shell exploded nearby. A jagged iron fragment tore through Tilghman's chest, killing him instantly.

Although most of Pemberton's defeated army safely crossed the Raymond road bridge, Loring and the 6,500 men of his division were cut off. Heading south through the thick woods and swamps bordering Baker's Creek, Loring searched in vain for a ford. Along the way he abandoned all of his artillery and most of his supplies. Eventually he turned east and, three days later, joined Johnston's army at Jackson. Though

Pemberton blamed Loring for the defeat at Champion's Hill, Johnston came to Loring's defense, and the errant general was never censured or otherwise punished.

The battlefield was a scene of carnage, littered with the bodies of soldiers and horses, the wreckage of cannon, and spent ammunition. It had been the bloodiest and most decisive engagement thus far in the Vicksburg Campaign. Grant reported 2,441 casualties, Pemberton 3,839. Each side had lost some 400 men killed outright, and many more would die of their wounds. Following the battle, as Alvin Hovey rode along the depleted ranks of his division, he spied the flag of his old regiment, the 24th Indiana. "Where are the rest of my boys?" he asked the few men gathered around the colors. "They are lying over there," replied a soldier, pointing to the corpse-strewn hillside. Hovey turned his horse and rode away, weeping.

To get his troops back to Vicksburg, Pemberton had to cross the Big Black River, 10 miles west of Champion's Hill. To cover the retreat, earthworks had been erected on the east bank near the town of Bovina, where the Southern Mississippi Railroad crossed the river. Pemberton sent the army's wagons on across the river, and placed a newly arrived Tennessee brigade, commanded by Brigadier General John C. Vaughn, behind the earthworks. General Stevenson's exhausted men, who had borne the brunt of the early fighting at Champion's Hill, were sent over the bridge as soon as they arrived; others crossed on a little river steamer. Safe on the other side, they fell to the ground and slept. Bowen's men, tired but alert, were added to the force defending the earthworks.

This was Pemberton's last hope of delaying Grant's march on Vicksburg, and he took pains to make his position a strong one. From a bow-shaped parapet of logs and cotton bales along the river, the defenders commanded a shallow bayou littered with fallen trees, and an open field beyond.

But as McClernand's men approached the defenses just after daybreak on Sunday, May 17, they were full of confidence, while the outnumbered Confederates, many of them still groggy with sleep, were sick of fighting. The main Federal attack was entrusted to a huge brigadier general named Michael Lawler, an Irish-born battler of awesome repute. Grant once said of him: "When it comes to just plain hard fighting, I would rather trust old Mike Lawler than any of them." Dana, reporting to Stanton, assessed Lawler a bit differently: "He is as brave

Confederate Brigadier General John S. Bowen, commanding a division of Missourians and Arkansans, led a furious counterattack that almost drove the Federals from Champion's Hill. Bowen was promoted to major general, but during the siege of Vicksburg he contracted dysentery and died in July 1863, at the age of 33.

Sewn by women of Vicksburg for Company I of the 28th Mississippi Cavalry, this flag was carried throughout the campaign by Lieutenant Sid Champion, on whose farm the Battle of Champion's Hill was fought.

as a lion, and has about as much brains."

At the Big Black River there was more need for courage than for brains, and the 250-pound Lawler quickly confirmed his reputation for valor. Galloping back and forth, he deployed his four regiments of Iowa and Wisconsin men at the northern end of the Confederate line and, without waiting for orders, launched a bayonet attack. It was a hot day, and he was fighting in his shirtsleeves. He wore his sword belt in its customary position, looped over his shoulder; his belly was too big for him to wear it around his waist. As Lawler charged ahead on his horse across the open field toward the bayou, his men raced after him. Lawler led them through what he described as "a terrible fire of musketry from the front and a galling fire from sharpshooters on the right."

Colonel William Kinsman of the 23rd Iowa was out ahead of his men, waving his sword, when he went down. Lawler, who saw him fall, recalled: "Struggling to his feet, he staggered a few paces to the front, cheered forward his men, and fell again, this time to rise no more, pierced through by a second ball." Lawler's regiments halted at

the edge of the bayou, poured a volley into the defenses, then splashed through the knee-deep water and onto the breastworks.

The exhausted, dispirited Southerners were in no condition to resist. Many men waved bits of cotton on their ramrods in token of surrender, while others hurried to get across the bridge before it was burned.

They were, in fact, still crossing when both the bridge and the little river steamer were ordered burned by Pemberton. A few men drowned trying to swim the river. Those left behind were taken prisoner. In all, the Confederates lost about 200 men killed and wounded, and 1,751 captured. Federal casualties — mostly Lawler's men — amounted to 39 killed, 237 wounded and three missing. Among the Union injured was Fred Grant; he had been nicked in the leg by a sharpshooter. When an officer asked him what was wrong, he replied with pardonable exaggeration: "I am killed."

Pemberton had ridden up from Bovina, where he had spent the night, just in time to see the end of the battle. He now ordered his men to fall back to Vicksburg, 12 miles to the west. As he rode off with one of his officers, he said bitterly: "Just thirty years ago I began my cadetship at the U.S. Military Academy. Today, the same date, that career is ended in disaster and disgrace."

With his enemy reeling, Grant hurriedly ordered four bridges constructed across the Big Black and pushed his men westward. Sherman had now arrived from Jackson, and Grant set out with him to the north of Vicksburg, to establish a base there on the bluffs, which the Confederates had recently abandoned. Both men were so eager, said Grant, that they galloped far ahead of their troops. At last they stood on the bluffs,

In an etching based on a sketch by a Union lieutenant, Federal reinforcements advance on the double in pursuit of Confederates retreating through the woods near Champion's Hill. The troops of Brigadier General Lloyd Tilghman (*right*) successfully defended the Confederate escape route from what survivors called the "hill of death." But Tilghman, the West Point-trained scion of a prominent Maryland family, was killed by an exploding shell.

where, Grant wrote, "Sherman had the pleasure of looking down from the spot coveted so much by him the December before."

Just then, Sherman turned to Grant and made a speech that so impressed Grant that he recalled it distinctly 25 years later. Until that minute, Sherman said, he had doubted the wisdom of Grant's strategy. "This, however," he said, "was the end of one of the greatest campaigns in history," even if Vicksburg should somehow elude capture.

It was a triumphant moment for the Federal forces, and an unspeakably gloomy and bewildering one for the Confederates — not only for the defeated soldiers but also for the stunned citizens of Vicksburg. It was a Sunday no one in that town would ever forget.

Vague rumors of the defeats had spread, and clusters of people gathered on corners after church. No one had any real news, but all suspected the worst. And then, wrote 27-year-old Mary Loughborough, wife of a Confederate staff officer, "in all the dejected uncertainty, the stir of horsemen and wheels began." At first just a few exhausted men drifted through the streets. "Soon," Mrs. Loughborough recalled, "straggler after straggler came by, then groups of soldiers worn and dusty with the long march."

The pathetic trickle began at about noon and quickly swelled to a flood. "Until late in the night," Emma Balfour, a doctor's wife, wrote in her diary, "the streets and roads were jammed with wagons, cannons, horses, men, mules, stock, sheep." The townspeople had seen much of war by now, but nothing like this. They brought out food and water for the weary men, and they asked helpless questions. "Where are you going?" one woman cried out to a passing soldier. "We are whipped," he responded grimly.

Another resident, Dora Miller, secretly supported the Union, but she was deeply moved by the sight of the beaten Confederates. They seemed to her to be "humanity in the last throes of endurance. Wan, hollow-eyed, ragged, footsore, bloody, the men limped along unarmed, but followed by siege-guns, ambulances, gun carriages, and wagons in aimless confusion."

Mixed in with the ragged remnants of the army were great numbers of frightened civilians from the countryside, fleeing the advancing Federals. Soldiers, refugees and townsfolk all had one thing in common: They knew whom to blame. "It's all Pemberton's fault," said one soldier after another. Wrote Emma Balfour: "I knew from all I saw and heard that it was want of confidence in the General commanding that was the cause of our disaster."

Pemberton was at that moment working furiously to stave off the approaching Federals. He had been urged by Johnston to evacuate Vicksburg and march to the northeast. "Instead of losing both troops and place," Johnston said, "we must save the troops." But Pemberton called a second council of war, and afterward reported to Johnston that his officers had voted unanimously against withdrawal. "I have decided to hold Vicksburg as long as possible," he said.

Pemberton still commanded a powerful force — some 30,000 men, fewer than Grant's 45,000, but more than enough to defend Vicksburg. And Johnston had about 20,000 troops near Jackson. Furthermore, most of the 10,000 troops Pemberton had left behind in Vicksburg were fresh. These men — the divisions commanded by Major Generals Martin L. Smith and John H. Forney — had been manning the defensive line

to the south of town. Now they marched into the city, past the beaten and bedraggled soldiers, to bolster the threatened sections of the line to the north and east. Some of the women came out to greet them, crying: "You'll stand by us and protect us, won't you?" And in response, wrote Mary Loughborough, "the men, who were fresh and lively, swung their hats, and promised to die for the ladies — never to run — never to retreat."

A seven-mile line of defense works had been constructed around the town, anchored at each end on the river. Winter rains had washed away some of the earthen emplacements, but now soldiers were put to work rebuilding. The effort had started while the dust was still settling at the Big Black River — and it was none too soon.

Grant, whose three corps were now arrayed before the town's defenses, suspected that the enemy's morale had been shattered. "I believed," Grant wrote, "he would not make much effort to hold Vicksburg."

But when Grant attacked on May 19, he received a rude welcome. In 48 hours an astonishing transformation had occurred among the Confederates. Protected by strong fortifications, strengthened by fresh troops, they had swiftly recovered their spirits — and their effectiveness.

Grant ordered an assault with all his forces: McClernand on the east, McPherson and Sherman on the north. McClernand's and McPherson's troops, some of whom were still hurrying into position as the attack began, had great difficulty advancing through the thick underbrush, felled trees and steep ravines; they were soon pinned down by Confederate fire. The burden of the attack fell on Sherman's XV Corps, which moved off from positions closer to the Con-

Heading for Vicksburg, Sherman's Federal corps crossed the Big Black River on the floating bridge above, one of four spans Union soldiers constructed overnight to replace the one burned by Pemberton's retreating Confederates. The bridge was supported by rubber pontoons that were inflated with hand bellows *(inset)*.

federate defenses at the north end of the line.

Even then, only the brigade commanded by Colonel Giles A. Smith made any headway. Ignoring a flesh wound in the hip, Smith led his five regiments against a Confederate strongpoint known as the Stockade Redan. Most of Smith's men were halted by the fire that scythed through their ranks, but the 116th Illinois and the 1st Battalion, 13th U.S. Infantry, managed to gain a foothold in a ditch north of the stockade. The 13th was Sherman's old Regular Army outfit, and one of its captains was his brother-in-law, Charles Ewing. Ewing seized the battalion colors after three men had fallen trying to plant the flag on the Confederate works. As he brought it back to his line, a Minié ball passed harmlessly through his hat and another wounded him in the hand, while the banner itself was pierced by 55 bullets.

Captain J. J. Kellogg, with the 113th Illinois of Smith's brigade, said he could see "the very sticks and chips, scattered over the ground, jumping under the hot shower of Rebel bullets." His men were pinned down all afternoon in canebrakes; as the hours passed, Confederate fire cut down cane stalks one at a time, Kellogg said, so that "they lopped gently on us." As darkness fell and provided cover, Kellogg's regiment fell back along with the other units that had been similarly pinned down. Grant had lost 942 men, Pemberton 250. It was now clear what the Federals were up against. "This is a death struggle," Sherman wrote his wife after the battle, "and will be terrible."

Grant kept his men busy for the next two days preparing siegeworks. On the northern front, Sherman needed to find a way across the deep ditch that blocked access to the Rebel works; he thought of a wooden bridge. Although it was after dark, he sent his men out to find lumber. They reported that there was indeed some lumber nearby — in the

In this watercolor by an unknown artist, Grant's army moves through a gap to assault the fortifications around Vicksburg *(background)*. The men are shown marching to the music of a horse-drawn band *(foreground)*, sometimes stepping over the bodies of comrades felled by enemy artillery.

form of a house. The trouble was that Grant was sleeping in it. After some high-level discussion, it was agreed that Grant must be awakened. When the situation was explained, Grant arose, dressed, and watched as his headquarters was disassembled and turned into a bridge across the moat.

Another vital construction project was the building of a road to the steamboat landing at Chickasaw Bluffs; the need for supplies was becoming urgent. For almost three weeks the Union soldiers had subsisted well enough off the populace of Mississippi. They had raided Southern kitchens, gardens, smokehouses, hen houses, wine cellars and gristmills. But there were too many mouths to feed, and the countryside was soon picked clean. For several days, food had been increasingly hard to come by.

While Grant was inspecting his lines, he heard a soldier nearby say in a low voice: "Hardtack." Then others, politely but firmly, let their general know that they were hungry. "In a moment," Grant wrote later, "the cry was taken up all along the line, 'Hardtack! Hardtack!' " He told the nearest men that when the supply road was finished there would be plenty of bread and coffee. The men cheered.

By all accounts, the soldiers themselves — most of whom had not been heavily engaged in the first attack on the city — wanted to make another try. One man reported: "They felt as if they could march straight through Vicksburg, and up to their waists in the Mississippi, without resistance." A 19-year-old sergeant, Osborne Oldroyd of the 20th Ohio, reflected this spirit. "We have come here to compel them to surrender," he declared, "and they cannot say us nay."

A carefully coordinated assault was set for

10 a.m. on Friday, May 22. Before the infantry attack, Grant ordered an artillery barrage from every battery in position. Simultaneously, skirmishers began sniping at the defenders and Porter's gunboats opened up on the Vicksburg entrenchments from the river. The firing lasted for four hours.

As the Federal batteries thundered away, the infantrymen girded for the assault. "Men congregated in little groups conversing in undertones," recalled C. D. Morris of the 33rd Illinois. "Letters conveying a last farewell to loved ones were hurriedly written. Officers, outwardly calm, but dreading the task before them, moved aimlessly about, anxiously consulting their timepieces."

Then at 10 a.m., "as if by magic," recalled Confederate General Stephen D. Lee, "every gun and rifle stopped firing. The silence was almost appalling." Breathless, the Confederates waited. "Suddenly," said Lee, "there seemed to spring almost from the bowels of the earth dense masses of Federal troops, in numerous columns of attack, and with loud cheers and huzzahs, they rushed forward at a run with bayonets fixed, not firing a shot, headed for every salient along the Confederate lines."

The defenders held their fire until the Federal soldiers were well within range. Then, said Lee, they "deliberately rose and stood in their trenches pouring volley after volley into the advancing enemy."

Among the charging Federals was Lieutenant Colonel Lysander Webb of the 77th Illinois. His regiment's objective was the so-called Railroad Redoubt, which guarded the passage of the Southern Mississippi through the town's eastern defenses. "Down into the abatis of fallen timber and brush we went," wrote Webb, "our comrades falling thickly on all sides of us. Still up the hill we pressed, through the brambles and brush, over the dead and dying — up, up we struggled, over logs, into ditches, clinging here to a bush to keep from falling backwards, and there to a thorny bramble — oh! that was a half hour which may God grant we shall never be called upon to experience again." Only a handful of Webb's regiment managed to reach their objective.

The 21st Iowa of General Lawler's brigade was also fighting its way toward the formidable Railroad Redoubt. Regimental Adjutant George Crooke recalled, "It was a tornado of iron on our left, a hurricane of shot on our right. We passed through the mouth of hell. Every third man fell, either killed or wounded." Eventually survivors from several units gained a foothold on the redoubt. The flags of the 48th Ohio and 77th Illinois were planted atop the parapet, and Sergeant J. E. Griffith of the 22nd Iowa led 12 men through an embrasure and into the work itself. But the Federal success was short-lived. The 30th Alabama mounted a counterattack that cleared the parapet. The flag of the 77th Illinois was torn from its staff and captured. Corporal Isaac Carmen of the 48th Ohio attempted to save his regimental colors. But as he scampered down the slope, he impaled his thigh on the bayonet of a fellow soldier huddled in the ditch below.

Just north of the Railroad Redoubt, Colonel Ashbel Smith and his 2nd Texas faced the onslaught of McClernand's Federals. "The earth," Smith wrote, was "black with their close columns." But the Texans were ready for them. Each of Smith's men had five loaded muskets at hand, and half his force stood ready to reload while the front rank fired. When the attackers came within 100 yards of the parapet, Smith gave the command to fire. "My cannon belched canister; my men made the air reel with yells and shouts as they saw the earth strewn with the enemy's dead." Soon the blazing musketry ignited the cotton bales lining the Confederate works, but the Texans' fire did not abate. It seemed that no Federal could cross that open space and live.

Suddenly, out of a pall of smoke came a lone blueclad figure, Private Thomas H. Higgins of the 99th Illinois, carrying the Stars and Stripes. "At least a hundred men took deliberate aim at him," a Texas private recalled, "but he never faltered. Stumbling over the bodies of his fallen comrades, he continued to advance." Awed by such suicidal courage, some Texans began shouting, "Don't shoot at that man!" while others cried, "Come on, you brave Yank!" Higgins carried his flag right up to the Confederate line, where he was pulled inside the works and captured. Word of his deed spread through the Confederate ranks, and that night he was brought before an admiring General Pemberton. Later, Higgins would be awarded the Medal of Honor, with a citation based in part on the testimony of his Confederate foes.

To the north, on Sherman's front, a 14-year-old drummer boy, Orion Howe of the 55th Illinois, embarked on a mission that would win him the Medal of Honor. When his regiment's ammunition ran low, Howe volunteered to go to the rear and order more. As he left, the 55th's commander, Colonel Oscar Malmborg, called out to the boy, reminding him to request .54-caliber ammunition, the only kind the regiment could use.

"We could see him nearly all the way," wrote a soldier of the 55th. "He ran through what seemed a hailstorm of canister and musket balls, each throwing up a little puff as it struck the dry hillside." Once the watchers despaired to see the youngster fall, but he had merely tripped. Finally he disappeared from sight.

Sherman, who was watching the battle, wrote later that "this young lad came up to me wounded and bleeding" — Howe had just been struck in the leg by a Minié ball. In clear tones, the boy delivered his message: "General Sherman, send some cartridges to Colonel Malmborg; the men are all out." Sherman promised to see to it, then hurried Howe off to a hospital. "Just before he disappeared," the general wrote, "he turned and called as loud as he could, 'Calibre .54.'"

By now, Grant's attack was floundering all along the line. In some cases soldiers refused to advance, despite the curses and entreaties of their officers. Those regiments that did go forward were pinned down in front of the Confederate works under a scorching sun. The men lay prone; to raise one's head was to die. "My thirst became intolerable," said Adjutant Crooke of the 21st Iowa, pinned down near the railroad tracks. Crooke spied a single unripe plum dangling from a bush 10 yards to his front. "As my lips became hot and parched and my throat struggled to relieve itself, this green plum hung temptingly before me and bade me risk my life for it. For a long time I resisted, but the long, weary hours prolonged themselves into eternities, the ground became hotter and the sun's rays more scorching." Finally Crooke made a mad dash for the plum as Confederate bullets whizzed past him. He reached his goal unscathed, noting that "the few drops of juice more than repaid me for the risk, and the sweetest morsel of fruit ever tasted

Climbing into a hail of Minié balls and grapeshot, a sergeant of the 22nd Iowa advances to plant his regiment's colors atop the Confederate breastworks of Fort Beauregard at Vicksburg. The Union attackers were ultimately driven back after suffering their heaviest losses of the campaign.

by man will live in my memory forever."

By early in the afternoon it was becoming abundantly clear to Grant that the assault was doomed. He was about to call a halt when he received a scrawled note from McClernand. "We have part possession of two forts and the Stars and Stripes are waving over them," McClernand wrote. "A vigorous push ought to be made all along the line." Grant, standing with Sherman, handed the note over and said, "I don't believe a word of it." Grant wrote later, "I believed I could see as well as he what took place in his front, and I did not see the success he reported." Still, more urgent requests followed the first, and Grant finally and reluctantly sent more troops to McClernand and ordered Sherman and McPherson to renew their attacks. They did so, and suffered heavy casualties. In the bitter words of Sergeant Aaron Dunbar of the 93rd Illinois, "It was much like marching men to their graves in line of battle." McClernand had lost his tenuous grip on the Confederate fortifications. He could not break through, and this failure would come back to haunt him.

For the Federals, the attack on Vicksburg on May 22 had been the bloodiest battle of the campaign. Grant's losses amounted to 3,199 men, 502 of whom had been killed. The Confederates had suffered fewer than 500 casualties.

As the sound of firing died down among the tortured Vicksburg hillsides that Friday, Grant sat on his horse whittling a piece of wood. It had been a savage day and a grueling week, and the Federal troops were still outside the fortifications of the river port. A newspaper reporter heard Grant say quietly: "We'll have to dig our way in."

Closing the Ring

"Proud as I was of my brave troops, honoring them, as I did, I felt that it would be an act of cruel inhumanity to subject them longer to the terrible ordeal. I saw no advantage to be gained by protracting a hopeless defense, which I knew must be attended with a useless waste of life and blood."

LIEUTENANT GENERAL JOHN C. PEMBERTON, C.S.A.

Although Vicksburg remained to be taken, Grant's successes had given him new confidence — and an unaccustomed celebrity. His superiors, his fellow officers, his soldiers and the Union public all hailed his achievements.

Newspapers filled their pages with Grant's praises. Horace Greeley's New York *Tribune*, which had hammered Grant mercilessly ever since Shiloh, now wrote in awe of the general's tireless, near-flawless campaigning. "Grant has scratched 'rest' out of his dictionary and moves right on as though impelled by a motive power which he could not resist," Greeley declared.

William Tecumseh Sherman drew a cynical lesson from the sudden change in his friend's public image. "Grant is now deservedly the hero," Sherman wrote his wife. "He is now belabored with praise by those who a month ago accused him of all the sins in the calendar, and who next week will turn against him if so blows the popular breeze." Sherman concluded caustically, "Vox populi, vox humbug."

The audacious May campaign had no more watchful analysts than the soldiers who fought it, and their approbation was evident. In a June dispatch, the correspondent of *The New York Times* wrote: "The soldiers observe him coming and, rising to their feet, gather on each side of the way to see him pass — they do not salute him, they only watch him curiously, with a certain sort of familiar reverence." Said a private: "Every-

thing that Grant directs is right. His soldiers believe in him."

General in Chief Halleck, who had treated Grant with icy reserve a few months before, now began eagerly to comply with his requests for reinforcements, sending Grant great numbers of men to help strengthen his hold on the river port. Among them were the 8,000 men of Major General John G. Parke's IX Corps, dispatched from the Department of the Ohio, and a division of 5,000 men from the Department of the Missouri.

The reinforcements were sorely needed. The Union ring around Vicksburg was 12 miles in length, and Grant's 50,000-man force was stretched thin. In fact, though Pemberton wrote Johnston on May 29 that escape from Vicksburg was impossible, two of the eight roads leading out of town were virtually unguarded by Federal troops.

That situation did not last long. Grant used the first of the reinforcements to plug the gaps a few days later, and soon had more than 70,000 men in his command. In this iron grip, a Confederate soldier observed grimly, "a cat could not have crept out of Vicksburg without being discovered."

Grant proceeded to lay siege to Vicksburg. As he put it, his strategy was simply to "outcamp the enemy" until their supplies gave out. He also intended to apply constant pressure: Artillery bombarded the Confederates around the clock, and the Union infantry kept pushing their lines clos-

Confederates behind a parapet at Vicksburg hurl lighted artillery shells down on Federal attackers in June 1863. The Federals, who had dug a trench to within 20 yards of the works, fight back with a weapon rarely used before in the War — a hand grenade. Among the primitive grenades employed was the three-pound, dartlike type above, which detonated on impact.

er to the town. Troops were sent out each night to dig approach trenches, or saps. These were constructed in the traditional zigzag pattern, to prevent the enemy from shooting straight down their length. The earth displaced by the digging was piled up on the side of the trench nearer the Confederates, and to provide further protection the earthworks were strengthened with cotton bales, sandbags and logs.

The art of laying siege called for some special equipment that Grant's army had not been furnished, but the general improvised ably. Lacking heavy siege guns, he bombarded the town with field artillery and with naval guns borrowed from Admiral Porter. Sap rollers — large cylindrical devices used to protect the trench diggers from enemy fire — were fashioned by weaving branches into large baskets and filling them with earth. Trench mortars were fabricated on the spot by shrinking iron bands around short lengths of tree trunks, which were then hollowed out to take 6- and 12-pound shells. A crude periscope for looking into the Confederate entrenchments was made by mounting a mirror on a pole.

"Every man in the investing line became an army engineer day and night," an infantryman wrote. "The soldiers got so they bored like gophers and beavers, with a spade in one hand and a gun in the other."

Confederate sharpshooters made the work hazardous, but the troops maintained a certain humor about it all. "A favorite amusement of the soldiers," a Federal officer said, "was to place a cap on the end of a ramrod and raise it just above the head-logs, betting on the number of bullets which would pass through it in a given time." As if the sharpshooters were not enough, the Con-

federates had an annoying habit of firing turpentine-soaked projectiles into the sap rollers, setting them afire and sending the diggers scurrying.

But the Federal forces inexorably pressed forward, until the lead trenches were within a few yards of the Confederate earthworks. As had happened before in this brother-against-brother war, the close proximity of the rival forces at a time when there was no immediate battle to fight fostered an interlude of reduced tension and even a kind of camaraderie. There was a steady interchange of shouted jokes and taunts between the Federal and Confederate soldiers. At one point, wrote Captain Samuel Byers of the 5th Iowa, "our lines were so close together that our pickets often had a cup of coffee or a chew of tobacco with the Rebel pickets at night. Drummer Bain, of my company, had a brother among the soldiers inside Vicksburg. One night he met him at the picket line, and together they walked all through the beleaguered town."

A favorite meeting place between the lines was an abandoned house that had a good well. There was a severe water shortage in both armies, and thirsty pickets from the two sides would congregate there. Sometimes they became engaged in heated political arguments, but when the discussions grew too vehement the groups would break off — as one man said, "to avoid a fight on the subject."

These good-humored exchanges notwithstanding, the siege was proceeding in earnest. On May 27, Grant had ordered Admiral Porter to send the ironclad gunboat *Cincinnati*, commanded by Lieutenant George M. Bache, down the Mississippi to bombard Fort Hill, the westernmost Con-

General Grant made three major attempts to storm the defenses that ringed Vicksburg. On May 19, Francis Blair's division and the 1st Battalion, 13th Infantry, advanced on the Stockade Redan but were pinned down in a timber-clogged ravine by enemy fire. Three days later, on May 22, men of McClernand's corps reached the parapet of the Railroad Redoubt. McClernand's troops were not able to sustain their drive, however, and were forced to pull back. On June 25, the Federals detonated explosives under the Confederate works near the Jackson road and charged through the resulting crater, but were again unable to sustain their attack.

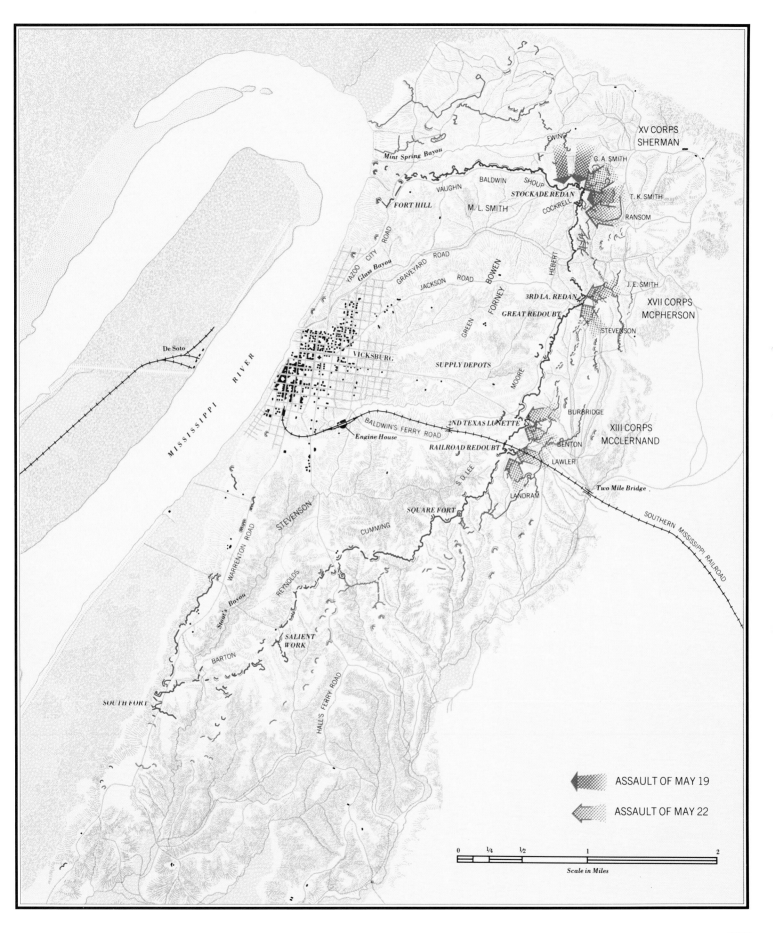

MISSISSIPPI RIVER

De Soto

XV CORPS
SHERMAN

EWING

G. A. SMITH

Mint Spring Bayou

BALDWIN   SHOUP
VAUGHN   STOCKADE REDAN   T. K. SMITH

FORT HILL   M. L. SMITH   COCKRELL   RANSOM

Glass Bayou
YAZOO CITY ROAD

GRAVEYARD ROAD
BOWEN
HEBERT
JACKSON   ROAD
FORNEY
J. E. SMITH

3RD LA. REDAN   XVII CORPS
GREAT REDOUBT   MCPHERSON
GREEN
STEVENSON

VICKSBURG

SUPPLY DEPOTS

MOORE

BURBRIDGE

2ND TEXAS LUNETTE
BALDWIN'S FERRY ROAD   BENTON   XIII CORPS
Engine House   MCCLERNAND
RAILROAD REDOUBT   LAWLER

S. D. LEE   Two Mile Bridge

STEVENSON   LANDRAM
WARRENTON ROAD   SQUARE FORT

CUMMING   SOUTHERN MISSISSIPPI RAILROAD

Stout's Bayou
REYNOLDS

SALIENT
WORK

BARTON

HALL'S FERRY ROAD

SOUTH FORT

ASSAULT OF MAY 19

ASSAULT OF MAY 22

0   1/4   1/2   1   2

Scale in Miles

Bombproofs excavated by the 45th Illinois to provide shelter from Confederate artillery riddle a hillside near the front outside Vicksburg. The white frame house belonged to a family who fled to a cave during the siege.

federate bastion at Vicksburg. Both Grant and Sherman believed mistakenly that the fort's battery of heavy guns had been moved elsewhere in the defenses. If the rifle pits there could be silenced, they reasoned, a way might be cleared for Sherman to smash through. But the current was so strong that the *Cincinnati* was forced to turn upstream to hold her position; in the process she exposed her unarmored stern to the Confederate batteries. She was hit repeatedly, and sank in 20 feet of water. Thirteen of her 200-man crew drowned, and 19 were killed or wounded by Confederate fire. The vessel was later burned by the Confederates, but her guns were recovered by Federal forces and added to those ringing the town.

By mid-June, more than 200 Union cannon were shelling Vicksburg from land while Porter directed frequent bombardments from the river. The targets of the Federal guns were unquestionably military — princi-

pally the Confederate entrenchments and their occupants. But it often seemed to the town's civilian inhabitants that they were the chief targets. The Confederate soldiers in trenches and behind breastworks were well protected; the civilians were more vulnerable, and shells fell all about them. "The general impression is that they fire at the city," wrote Emma Balfour, "in that way thinking that they will wear out the women and children and sick; and General Pemberton will be impatient to surrender the place on that account." The officer husband of Mary Loughborough grew so concerned about her welfare in the town that he moved her and their child to a safer place — up to the front.

The people under bombardment were ill-prepared to endure it, and there was scarcely any relief. The gunboats alone fired a total of 22,000 shells at the town's defenses, and the barrage from the army's batteries was even heavier.

Very early in the siege, the Vicksburgers concluded that there was no safety in their houses, and they began burrowing into the hillsides. "Caves were the fashion — the rage," remarked Mary Loughborough. By the end of the siege, roughly 500 caves had been dug in the yellow clay hills of Vicksburg. One woman remarked that the place was "so honeycombed with caves that the streets look like avenues in a cemetery." Federal soldiers began calling Vicksburg "Prairie Dog Village."

Although some people used the caves simply as bomb shelters, many lived in them permanently. The temporary shelters, one visitor observed, might be "no larger than a fireplace." But the permanent refuges could be almost luxurious — many-roomed

Sheltered in a cave dug by slaves, a Vicksburg woman kneels in prayer. Like many other residents, she made her underground dwelling as homey as possible with furniture and rugs.

dwellings equipped with furniture brought from the houses, and with rugs covering the dirt floors. Some had clay walls separating their chambers, with doors fitted into them for privacy.

Even in the best of circumstances, however, cave life was far from pleasant. For some people, the sense of confinement was even worse than the menace of falling shells. "Sometimes," said a man interviewed by Mark Twain after the War, "the caves were desperately crowded, and always hot and close. Sometimes a cave had twenty or twenty-five people packed into it; no turning room for anybody; air so foul, sometimes, you couldn't have made a candle burn in it. A child was born in one of those caves one night. Think of that; why, it was like having it born in a trunk."

Horror stories proliferated about the effects of the bombardment on the residents, and whether true or not, these tales helped undermine morale. Mark Twain was told of a man who was shaking hands with a friend when an exploding shell suddenly left him holding a disembodied hand. The diarist Mary Boykin Chesnut, in faraway Richmond, heard about a three-year-old girl who was struck by a shell: "There was this poor little girl with her touchingly lovely face, and her arm gone." Mary Loughborough told of a woman who had put her infant to sleep in a cave and was sitting near the entrance to the shelter when a mortar shell smashed through the dirt roof and crushed the baby to death.

Despite such accounts, the danger to the inhabitants of the town was more apparent than real. Fewer than a dozen civilians were known to have been killed during the entire siege, and perhaps three times that

Young Lucy McRae of Vicksburg was buried alive when an exploding Federal shell collapsed part of a cave in which she had taken refuge. She was quickly rescued by fellow cave dwellers, including the Reverend William W. Lord (*above*), and suffered no serious injury.

number were injured. Still, thousands had to endure the torment of living day after day under siege.

The people of Vicksburg expected a rescue attempt at any time. So did Grant. On May 29 he had received a letter from Banks asking him to send 10,000 men downriver to assist in the ongoing siege of Port Hudson. "Of course I could not comply with his request," Grant wrote later, "nor did I think he needed them. He was in no danger of an attack by a garrison on his front, and there was no army organizing in his rear to raise the siege."

Grant, on the other hand, did have an enemy army organizing in his rear. Joseph E. Johnston, now encamped at Jackson, was reportedly raising an army of between 30,000 and 40,000 men, and he worried the Union commander. "General Grant told me,"

A Confederate soldier and two women in a Vicksburg lane shrink in horror at the sight of a Federal shell with a sputtering fuse. "While comparatively few non-combatants were killed," one resident wrote, "all lived in a state of terror."

Sherman said, "that Johnston was about the only general on that side whom he feared."

Grant also knew perfectly well what Johnston was thinking. When an officer suggested that the Confederate general might be planning to enter Vicksburg with 30,000 men to help Pemberton break the siege, Grant said: "No. We are the only fellows who want to get in there. The rebels who are in now want to get out, and those who are out want to stay out." He went on: "If Johnston tries to cut his way in we will let him do it, and then see that he don't get out. You say he has 30,000 men with him? That will give us 30,000 more prisoners than we now have."

What Grant did fear — and what Johnston was hoping to mount — was an attack on the Federal rear that would give Pemberton a chance to break out and join Johnston.

Grant thought it necessary, therefore, not only to pin down the Confederates in Vicksburg but to establish what he described as "a second line of defense facing the other way." Four weeks into the siege, one division from each of the three Federal corps was detached to form an independent force under Sherman's command, with orders to guard against any approach by Johnston across the Big Black River.

Johnston, meanwhile, faced a cruel dilemma. Although his forces had been strengthened, and were aching to fight, Grant's army still outnumbered Johnston's and Pemberton's together. "Johnston evidently took in the situation," Grant wrote long afterward, "and wisely, I think, abstained from making an assault on us because it would simply have inflicted loss on both sides without accomplishing any result."

In any case, a combined Confederate attack appeared almost impossible to coordinate. Communications between Johnston and Pemberton had become exceedingly difficult. Couriers were sent out repeatedly by both Confederate commanders. Some tried to cross the lines by slipping through gullies and woodlands, while others traveled by boat or canoe along the Yazoo and Mississippi Rivers in hopes of skirting the enemy. Few made it.

The messages Johnston did get through to Pemberton made vague pledges of aid: "Bragg is sending a division. When it comes I will move to you." But to Richmond, Johnston confided his worst fears: "I have not at my disposal half the troops needed to relieve Vicksburg." And in another dispatch: "I consider saving Vicksburg hopeless."

Secretary of War James Seddon responded to Johnston's pessimism with something approaching horror. "Your telegram grieves and alarms us," he wired on June 16. "Vicksburg must not be lost, at least without a struggle. The interest and honor of the Confederacy forbid it. I rely on you still to avert the loss." Seddon urged Johnston to attack — with Pemberton or without him. Four days later, Seddon tried again. "Rely upon it," he wrote Johnston, "the eyes and hopes of the whole Confederacy are upon you, with the full confidence that you will act, and with the sentiment that it were better to fail nobly daring than, through prudence even, to be inactive."

When the campaign for Vicksburg began, Johnston had been one of the most admired generals in the South. But weeks of inaction had eroded his popularity, and a sharp note of criticism crept into newspaper assessments of this commander. "He has done no more," complained the Richmond *Sentinel*, "than to sit by and see Vicksburg fall and

Advancing on the Confederate defenses around Vicksburg, Federal sappers construct a shielded approach roofed with protective bundles of wood called fascines, strong enough to withstand artillery fire. In the foreground, a crew cuts and ties together poles for the fascines.

send in the news." A reporter for the Mobile *Register* wrote acidly that Johnston was "fighting Grant daily by giving him 'a terrible letting alone.' " And still the ailing Johnston waited and worried.

With no one to fight, Grant found himself with time on his hands. By the end of May, the siege had settled into a routine that did not require his constant attention. And during this respite, according to an account by journalist Sylvanus Cadwallader that did not appear until after Grant's death, the general's old nemesis — his fondness for alcohol — reasserted itself.

A reputation for periodic overindulgence in whiskey had dogged Grant since he had resigned from the Army in 1854 — allegedly to avoid a court-martial for drunkenness on duty. His offense had been neither unusual nor particularly serious (hard drinking was an occupational hazard in the Regular Army), but as Grant rose to prominence, the charge shadowed him. In fact, allegations that he had been drunk at Shiloh had nearly ended his Army career again.

Grant does seem to have liked alcohol and to have had a poor head for it. There is ample testimony that he never took the field while under the influence of liquor. But when his attention was not fully occupied, and when he was away from his wife, he turned from time to time to alcohol for comfort.

Sylvanus Cadwallader wrote of being in the tent of the army's chief of artillery, Colonel William S. Duff, on the night of May 12, 1863 when Grant quietly emerged out of the darkness and asked Duff for a drink. Duff did not rise from his cot, but reached under his pillow for a flask and poured Grant "a generous portion" in a tin cup; Grant "swallowed it with great apparent satisfaction." Cadwallader got the impression that this had not been the general's first such visit.

Then, in the first week of June, Cadwallader was present for a two-day interlude during which Grant indulged in an extended drinking spree. According to the respected journalist's detailed account, the affair occurred on a short trip up the Yazoo River to a small town called Satartia to inspect one of Sherman's divisions. On board the steamer *Diligent*, Grant made several trips to the bar and, said Cadwallader, "became stupid in speech and staggering in gait." The keen-eyed observer Charles Dana, also aboard the steamer, reported later only that the general "was ill and went to bed soon after we started."

The inspection was forgotten and the steamer returned during the night to a landing just above Vicksburg. On arising, Grant, to Cadwallader's horror, somehow proceeded to get drunk again and demanded to be put ashore a few miles away at Chickasaw Bayou, where Sherman had been defeated the previous December. It was now a bustling Federal supply depot, and Grant's ap-

pearance at the crowded docks, Cadwallader remarked, could have led "to utter disgrace and ruin."

Cadwallader managed to delay the landing, with the connivance of the *Diligent's* captain, until sunset. During the docking, the reporter lost track of the general, only to find him after a while in a nearby sutler's tent, where he was drinking with a jovial group of officers.

Cadwallader implored the general to mount up, join his escort and return to headquarters. When Grant reached his horse, he leaped on and galloped away before anyone could stop him. Grant, a superb horseman, went tearing down a winding road at full speed, past astonished sentries, cutting across fields and running, as Cadwallader put it, "literally through and over everything in his way." Continued Cadwallader: "The air was full of dust, ashes and embers from campfires, and shouts and curses from those he rode down in his race." Behind him, like the tail to a comet, came Cadwallader on his own horse, followed by the mounted escort, trying desperately to catch up with the man they were supposed to guard.

Grant finally slowed to a walk, and when Cadwallader overtook him, he persuaded the general to dismount and lie down in the grass off the trail. There Grant quickly went to sleep. Cadwallader flagged one of the soldiers from the escort, told him to find Grant's chief of staff—no one else—and have him send an ambulance.

Grant's chief of staff was a young Galena lawyer, now a lieutenant colonel, named John A. Rawlins. Rawlins' father had been an alcoholic, and the son grew up with an aversion to alcohol. He appointed himself watchman over Grant's conduct, and chided the general in a manner that sometimes appalled the other members of Grant's staff. "He bossed everything at Grant's headquarters," Charles Dana wrote. "I have heard him curse at Grant when, according to his judgment, the general was doing something that he thought he had better not do." Rawlins, said an officer, was guilty of "insubordination twenty times a day." The only one who did not seem offended was Grant.

Rawlins received Cadwallader's message that night and dispatched an ambulance. "We reached headquarters about midnight," Cadwallader wrote, "and found Rawlins and Colonel John Riggin waiting for us at the driveway." Riggin was one of Grant's senior aides-de-camp. "I stepped out of the ambulance first," the reporter went on, "and was followed promptly by Grant. He shrugged his shoulders, pulled down his vest, 'shook himself together,' as one just rising from a nap, and seeing Rawlins and Riggin, bid them goodnight in a natural tone and manner, and started to his tent as steadily as he ever walked in his life.

"My surprise nearly amounted to stupefaction. I turned to Rawlins and said I was afraid he would think I was the man who had been drunk."

But Rawlins replied through clenched teeth: "No, no. I know him, I know him."

The reporter spent a sleepless night, and avoided Grant the following day. But when he finally encountered the general, not a word was said about the incident — nor was it ever mentioned later by any of the other witnesses. Washington received not a hint of the episode.

Whatever personal difficulties Grant was wrestling with that June, he managed to clear up a problem among his staff that had been hanging over the army since the pre-

Clash at Milliken's Bend

Before dawn on June 7, 1863, a force of 1,500 Texans commanded by Brigadier General Henry E. McCulloch approached the Federal outpost at Milliken's Bend, a short distance above Vicksburg on the Louisiana side of the Mississippi. The outpost was manned by 1,061 troops — one regiment of whites and three regiments of recently recruited black soldiers, known as the African Brigade.

Sensing an easy victory, McCulloch's Con-

federates charged, shouting, "No quarter!" A desperate hand-to-hand struggle ensued. The outnumbered Federals, wielding bayonets and using their guns as clubs, contested each foot of territory as they were driven back toward the Mississippi. Many of the Union soldiers fell before the Texans; others were captured.

Then the tide of battle suddenly shifted. Two Federal gunboats dispatched from upriver by Admiral Porter began to pour

fire into the Confederate ranks, compelling them to retreat.

Of the 652 Federals lost at Milliken's Bend, 566 were from the black regiments. Most of the freedmen taken prisoner during the battle were returned to slavery. But the bravery of those troops left an indelible impression on their fellow Federals. An admiring officer declared: "I never more wish to hear the expression 'The Niggers won't fight.'"

Black troops of the so-called African Brigade clash with Confederates at Milliken's Bend. A Northern reporter who viewed the mangled bodies left on the battlefield declared the contest "the most desperate of the War."

vious autumn. John A. McClernand was still treating the War as a showcase for his ambitions. He missed no opportunity to claim credit for himself, warranted or not, and his posturing and near-insubordination had earned him powerful enemies throughout Grant's army. McClernand was suspected of antedating letters to make it appear that the successful ideas of others had been his in the first place. Grant had been tempted to remove McClernand more than once — most recently after a confrontation between the Illinois politician and Grant's youthful and energetic inspector general, Lieutenant Colonel James H. Wilson.

Wilson had been sent by Grant to order McClernand to contribute his share of troops to the force under Sherman that was watching for Johnston. When Wilson delivered the order, McClernand exploded. "I'll be God damned if I'll do it!" he cried. "I am tired of being dictated to. I won't stand it any longer, and you can go back and tell General Grant!" He added a few more expletives.

Wilson, white-lipped, retorted: "It seems to me that you are cursing me as much as you are cursing General Grant. If this is so, although you are a major general, and I am only a lieutenant colonel, I will pull you off that horse and beat the boots off of you!"

McClernand suddenly cooled down. "I was merely expressing my intense vehemence on the subject matter, sir," he said stiffly, "and I beg your pardon."

Wilson reported the incident to Grant verbatim. "I'll get rid of McClernand the first chance I get," Grant assured Wilson. But the commander was also somewhat tickled by the story. He never used profanity himself. (Dana once saw the general's horse stumble so badly in the darkness that Grant was al-

most thrown. "Now he will swear," thought Dana. But Grant merely rode on, Dana noted, "without a word or sign of impatience.") Chief of Staff Rawlins, on the other hand, abstemious though he might be, was violently profane. The next time Rawlins swore, Grant looked up, amused, and said to the other members of his staff: "He's not cursing. He is simply expressing his intense vehemence on the subject matter."

In mid-June, one of Sherman's division commanders, Major General Francis Preston Blair Jr., showed him a story in the Memphis *Evening Bulletin* that quoted a congratulatory general order McClernand had distributed to his troops following the assault of May 22. In this document McClernand took full credit for the initial achievements that day, and implied that his corps would have carried the Confederate fortifications had it not been for the failure of McPherson and Sherman to give him adequate support.

Sherman was outraged. McClernand's proclamation, he told Grant, not only did an injustice to the rest of the troops in Grant's army, but was "an effusion of vain-glory and hypocrisy." McPherson, too, protested angrily, declaring that McClernand's order was a self-serving political document intended "to impress the public mind with the magnificent strategy, superior tactics and brilliant deeds" of its author.

McClernand had finally gone too far. Not only had he offended his fellow officers; he had published an official order without the knowledge of his commanding officer, a violation of Army regulations. On June 18, Grant wrote an order relieving McClernand from command of his corps and sending him back to Illinois to await further instructions.

Colonel Wilson had the satisfaction of de-

livering the order to McClernand personally. He put on his best uniform, arrived at McClernand's headquarters at 2 a.m. and demanded to see the general. McClernand must have guessed what was coming: Wilson found him seated at the field desk in his tent, wearing his full-dress uniform. McClernand read the paper Wilson handed him and exclaimed: "Well sir! I am relieved!" Then he looked up, doubtless caught the triumphant glint in Wilson's eye and rose to the occasion with a pun. "By God, sir," McClernand said, "we are both relieved!"

He was replaced by a tough old Regular, Major General E.O.C. Ord, and was not seen again in the Army of the Tennessee.

About the time of McClernand's departure, all of Grant's soldiers with coal-mining experience were ordered to report to Cap-

tain Andrew Hickenlooper, chief engineer of XVII Corps. On June 23, the 35 men who turned up were put to work digging a tunnel toward the Confederate entrenchments northeast of town. In only two days, the Federals excavated a gallery 45 feet long; from it three smaller tunnels radiated out another 15 feet directly under the Confederate redan north of the road to Jackson. On June 25 these tunnels were packed with 2,200 pounds of gunpowder.

The Confederates above the tunnels, men of the 3rd Louisiana and 43rd Mississippi, had heard the sound of digging and had surmised what was happening. They had then started a countermine with the help of some black laborers, hoping to break into the Federal tunnel and drive the foe away before any damage could be done.

They were still digging when the charges

Under the command of Major General John A. Logan (*right*), the 45th Illinois charges into a vast crater blasted out of the Confederate earthworks by a Federal mine on June 25. Confederate Brigadier General Louis Hébert reported that his soldiers had anticipated the explosion and that it created "no dismay or panic among those defending the line."

148

planted by the Federals went off on the afternoon of June 25. Six Confederate soldiers were killed by the explosion, and one of the blacks was thrown into the air and hurled all the way into the Federal position, where he landed unhurt.

The blast blew off a large chunk of the Confederate redan, leaving a crater in its place. While the dust was still settling, Brigadier General Mortimer D. Leggett's Federal brigade charged into the crater. But most of the Confederate troops, anticipating an explosion, had pulled back to a new line, and they were waiting. "As we went into the crater," Private Wilbur Crummer of the 45th Illinois recalled, "they met us with a terrible volley of musketry." The attackers pressed on beyond the breach in the redan, but then they encountered cannon fire. "The line," remembered Private Crummer, "wavers, staggers, and then falls back to the crater."

As the charge faltered, the Confederate 6th Missouri counterattacked. "A hand-to-hand conflict rages for hours," Crummer wrote. "Hand grenades and loaded shells are lighted and thrown over the parapet as you would play ball." General Leggett reported that "scarcely a grenade was thrown without doing damage, and in most instances horribly mangling those they happened to strike." General Logan, who was watching the battle, cried out, "My God! They are killing my bravest men in that hole!" Yet the Federal forces held on tenaciously to their position in the crater for three days. Finally, at 5 p.m. on June 28, they fell back to their own trenches. Federal losses totaled nearly 200, with 68 of them from the 45th Illinois. The Confederates lost fewer than 100 men.

On July 1 the Federals exploded another mine beneath the same redan. It did considerably more damage to the fortifications than the previous attempt. Twelve Confederates, including the commander of the 2nd Missouri, were killed and 108 wounded in the explosion and the ensuing artillery barrage. But the Federal officers were now more cautious, and they concluded that the blast had not been devastating enough to justify another assault.

In any case, it was growing increasingly clear — to both the Confederates and the Federals — that the fall of Vicksburg was only a matter of days. Federal sharpshooters were taking a mounting toll of the defenders. On June 27, Brigadier General Martin Green, who had been slightly wounded during the fight at the crater, was looking over the parapet of the redan when he was shot through the head and killed.

Like the people of Vicksburg, the Confederate soldiers were cramped, exhausted — and hungry. The troops had been getting inadequate rations since the siege began. The men who retreated to Vicksburg were receiving only one third of the meat and two thirds of the cornmeal that regulations prescribed. And shortages of such staples as salt and coffee had plagued everybody in Vicksburg for months. A British observer, Lieutenant Colonel James Fremantle, had noted in early May that Mississippians were drinking "a peculiar mixture called Confederate coffee, made of rye, meal, Indian corn or sweet potatoes." Salt was so hard to obtain that Vicksburg residents who owned smokehouses had pulled up the floors to extract the salt left from the meat-curing process over the years.

Pemberton had made sure that as his

forces were falling back from the Big Black River, all available livestock was herded in the same direction. "All cattle, sheep and hogs belonging to private parties, and likely to fall into the hands of the enemy, should be driven into our lines," he instructed. But once the livestock was gone — and it did not take long — the food shortage in Vicksburg became severe.

All sorts of substitutes were tried. The one item that was in fairly good supply was peas. Soon after the siege got under way, soldiers began eating a bread made of ground peas, and the civilians followed suit. It was aw-ful — either rubbery or hard as rock, and in either case foul-tasting.

Women went into the fields and gathered tender cane shoots to cook for their children. The soldiers, too, scrounged about, collecting blackberries, tree buds and weeds, and mixing them with half-ripe peaches to make a sort of stew.

When all the beef, pork and lamb had disappeared, townspeople and soldiers alike turned, with great hesitation, to other meat. Chaplain William Foster saw some soldiers butchering "what I at first thought was beef." Not until he took a second look at the

Federal soldiers surge through the crater opened by explosives in the Confederate line on June 25. The attackers, according to one Federal who witnessed the effort, fought desperately "until their guns were too hot for further use." They gained a toehold and clung to it for three days, but finally were beaten back.

carcass did he notice "a head with long ears." It was a mule. The commissary sold the mule meat to civilians at a dollar a pound, and issued it free to those soldiers who wanted it. Many did not, but one of Pemberton's soldiers pronounced the meat "coarse-grained and darker than beef, but really delicious, sweet and juicy."

Some people also tried horse flesh. One Vicksburg resident wrote of seeing an officer's mount struck and severely injured by shellfire. The officer was forced to kill his horse on the spot. After the officer left, the resident saw a soldier "stop at the carcass, wait a moment and then deliberately commence to cut him off a large chunk."

As the siege wore on and hunger spread, several observers noted that dogs — which earlier had run through the streets howling during every bombardment — had all but disappeared, along with cats.

The townspeople made fun of their plight. During the siege, handwritten advertising cards appeared in Vicksburg trumpeting the virtues of the fictitious Hotel de Vicksburg: "Parties arriving by the river or Grant's overland route will find Grape, Cannister & Co.'s carriages at the landing." The establishment's menu, decorated with a picture of a mule's head, featured such dishes as "Mule Tail Soup, Mule Foot Jelly, Mule Tongue cold a la bray, Pea Meal Pudding and Genuine Confederate Coffee." One of the beverages listed was "Mississippi Water vintage 1492 Superior."

The shortage of water was, in fact, a serious problem in the besieged town, despite the proximity of the great river. The Mississippi was too filthy to drink, and most water supplies were drawn from a limited number of wells and springs, whose capacity was soon strained by the presence of so many soldiers. Guards were posted at the wells to keep troops from wasting water "for purposes of cleanliness."

Privation in Vicksburg did not fall upon all the besieged soldiers and civilians equally. Some men in uniform had access to food supplies, and made the most of it. Major William Drennan shared living space with a commissary officer, and while others were going hungry he ate, according to his diary, "good beef, mutton sometimes, ham, flour, rice flour, rice, molasses, etc." Wealthy civilians were able to buy food from profiteers — when those individuals had something to sell. Said Chaplain Foster: "Molasses was ten dollars a gallon, flour five dollars a pound & meal one hundred and forty dollars per bushel, and, none to be had scarcely at that."

Sergeant William Tunnard of the 3rd Louisiana almost sputtered as he wrote about the speculators. "These bloodsuckers," he said, "had the audacity to hold their goods at such prices that it was an utter impossibility to obtain anything from them. Some of these, worse than villains, refused to sell to the soldiers at any price."

Early in the siege, when speculation already was rampant, some of the victims took their revenge. On the night of June 1, an entire block of stores in the heart of the town, including a number of shops owned by alleged speculators, had been burned to the ground. The fire caused the worst damage suffered in the town during the siege, and everyone knew why it had happened.

As the siege wore on, morale in the town began to droop noticeably. "I have read of besieged cities and the sufferings of the inhabitants," wrote Army surgeon Joseph Alison in his diary, "but always thought the picture too highly painted. But now I have witnessed one and can believe all that is written on the subject."

Said Dora Miller, the Unionist trapped in Vicksburg with her husband: "I have never understood before the full force of these questions — what shall we eat? what shall we drink? and wherewithal shall we be clothed?"

The plight of the troops was just as bad. By the end of June, the Confederate soldiers' ration had been reduced to one biscuit plus a couple of mouthfuls of bacon per day, and Federal soldiers, calling across the trenches, were twitting the Rebels about the arrival of their new general — General Starvation.

That month Chaplain Foster wrote a heartfelt lament for his suffering brothers-in-arms. "How long shall the endurance of our men be tested?" he asked. "Who ever heard of men lying in ditches day and night, exposed to the burning sun and drenching rains for a period of thirty days, and that too under continual fire and on quarter rations? Their limbs become stiff; their strength is frittered away; their flesh leaves their limbs and the muscles relax, and their eyes become hollow and their cheeks sunken. Their clothes are covered with dirt and — oh, horrible! — their bodies are occupied by filthy vermin." And perhaps most onerous of all, Foster added, "They have waited for Johnston so long that hope deferred makes the heart sick."

With the Confederates' will to resist visibly weakening, Grant decided to launch another all-out assault. He scheduled it for the morning of July 6. By an odd coincidence, General Johnston, at last convinced that he must try something, began during the first

week of July to move toward Vicksburg with the intention of attacking Grant. He hoped to save Pemberton's army; Vicksburg he considered lost. He scheduled his attack for July 7.

But events were now moving faster than either general's plans. On July 1, Pemberton sent a message to his four division commanders: Major Generals Carter L. Stevenson, Martin Luther Smith, John H. Forney and John S. Bowen. "Unless the siege of Vicksburg is raised or supplies are thrown in," he wrote, "it will become necessary very shortly to evacuate the place. I see no prospect of the former, and there are many great, if not insuperable, obstacles in the way of the latter. You are, therefore, requested to inform me with as little delay as possible as to the condition of your troops, and their ability to make the marches and undergo the fatigues necessary to accomplish a successful evacuation."

The response was unanimous: Not one of the four commanders thought that a successful evacuation was possible. The reason was not lack of food, Pemberton wrote later; it was simply that the men were exhausted — "overpowered by numbers, worn down with fatigue."

There was only one course now open to Pemberton. On July 3, a day of scorching heat, he sent a message to Grant under a flag of truce. The bearer was General John Bowen, Grant's former St. Louis neighbor. Bowen was dying of dysentery but undertook this last errand in the hope that his friendship with Grant would count for something at such a critical moment.

The firing ceased. Heads appeared above the parapets on both sides, and the soldiers watched, transfixed, as General Bowen was

Soldiers of the 1st Battery, Wisconsin Light Artillery, stand beside their cannon outside Vicksburg. Lacking siege guns, Grant had to rely on light artillery to shell the town's defenses.

met by the Union's General Andrew Jackson Smith between the lines.

"I have the honor to propose to you an armistice for several hours," Pemberton's message to Grant read, "with a view to arranging terms for the capitulation of Vicksburg." Pemberton added that he was making the suggestion "to save the further effusion of blood, which must otherwise be shed to a frightful extent, feeling myself fully able to maintain my position for a yet indefinite period."

Grant accepted the message but declined to negotiate with Bowen. His reply to Pemberton was unyielding. "The useless effusion of blood you propose stopping by this course can be ended at any time you may

choose, by an unconditional surrender of the city and the garrison," he said. Then he softened the curt tone with an honest tribute. "Men who have shown so much endurance and courage as those now in Vicksburg will always challenge the respect of an adversary, and I can assure you will be treated with all the respect due to prisoners of war." He did agree, at Bowen's suggestion, to meet with Pemberton later that day.

The meeting between Pemberton and Grant was held at 3 p.m. Hundreds of soldiers watched, lying silently on the earthworks. Pemberton walked out accompanied by General Bowen and Colonel L. M. Montgomery. Grant was escorted by his staff and Generals Ord, McPherson, Logan and

The Risky Techniques of a Combat Artist

THEODORE DAVIS

Traveling with Grant's army during the Vicksburg Campaign was a 23-year-old artist for *Harper's Weekly*, Theodore Davis, who took extraordinary risks to achieve authenticity in his work. "To really see a battle," he wrote, "one must accept the most dangerous situations. It is only by going over the actual ground during the battle that one can decide what were its most interesting features."

In the field, and frequently under fire, Davis made hasty, rough sketches with notes. Later, in less hazardous surroundings, he used pen and ink to expand the sketches into detailed illustrations, such as the ones on these pages.

Theodore Davis paid a price for getting so close to the action. By the end of the War he had been wounded twice — once so seriously that he had to hold off surgeons at gunpoint to keep them from amputating his leg. Yet despite his wounds he was one of the conflict's most prolific artists, with more than 250 published drawings to his credit.

GRANT'S ARRIVAL IN VICKSBURG

SOLDIER FIRING A WOODEN MORTAR

DWELLINGS WRECKED BY SHELLFIRE

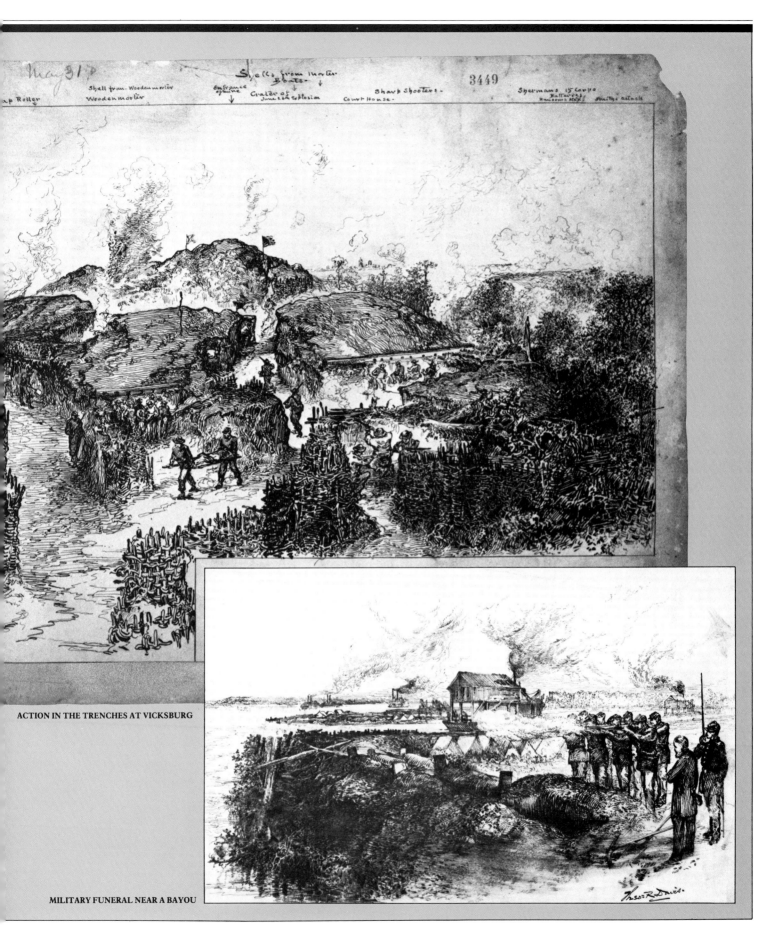

Shell from Wooden mortar

Wooden mortar

Entrance of mine

Crater of June 25th Explosion

Sharp Shooters

Court House

Sherman's 15 Corps
Battery Ransom's Mex

Smith's attack

ACTION IN THE TRENCHES AT VICKSBURG

MILITARY FUNERAL NEAR A BAYOU

Smith. The commanders met under a little tree 200 feet from the Confederate trenches.

It was a stiff, uncomfortable encounter. The generals shook hands, but Pemberton was uneasy and bitter, clearly hating every moment of the ordeal. When Grant told him there were no terms to discuss beyond what was in his note, Pemberton snapped, "The conference might as well end," and turned away abruptly. "Very well," Grant replied. But Bowen quickly intervened and suggested that he conduct further negotiations with some of Grant's officers. The two commanders agreed, and they strolled between the earthworks, chatting, while their subordinates talked over the next step and their troops watched from the opposing lines. At last it was decided that Grant's final terms would be sent to Pemberton at 10 p.m., and the two commanders departed.

Despite his firmness during the meeting, Grant in the end offered terms that stopped well short of unconditional surrender, and that later caused some controversy in the North. The dispute revolved around a provision allowing the Confederate soldiers to be paroled instead of being held prisoner; that is, they would be released upon signing an oath not to fight again until Federal captives were freed in exchange.

The parole offer, Grant said afterward, was made not as a gesture of good will, but for purely pragmatic reasons. "Had I insisted upon unconditional surrender," he said, "there would have been over 30,000 men to transport to Cairo, very much to the inconvenience of the army on the Mississippi." As it was, Grant felt confident that many of those paroled would desert and never return to the Confederate ranks. As he put it, "I knew many of them were tired of the war."

Sometime after midnight, Pemberton sent Grant a message accepting his terms. Grant, sitting in his tent with his son Fred, read the note and spoke quietly to the boy. "Vicksburg has surrendered," he said. It was the 48th day of the siege.

In the aftermath of the capitulation, many loose ends remained. Sherman had been waiting anxiously to the east of Vicksburg for word that he was free to drive against Johnston. That general, advancing cautiously toward the town with an army of 30,000 men, was increasingly puzzled by the silence from Vicksburg. When word of the surrender reached him on July 5, he hastily pulled back, with Sherman and his 40,000 troops right behind him.

Sherman pursued Johnston eastward past the recent battle sites at the Big Black River bridge and Champion's Hill, and back into Jackson. On the night of July 16, Johnston evacuated the capital and withdrew north into the Confederate heartland. Sherman, having successfully removed the last Confederate threat to Vicksburg, let him go.

In Vicksburg, meanwhile, the defeated troops had stacked their arms, and the town was taken over by Federal troops. Almost the first act of the victorious commander was to feed the stricken city. After the bulk of the Confederate forces had been bottled up at Vicksburg, Grant had been able to open his supply line from Grand Gulf, and now he brought up foodstuffs and poured them into the city. When the Federal soldiers arrived, their behavior was impeccable. "No word of exultation was uttered to irritate the feelings of the prisoners," wrote the Confederates' Sergeant Tunnard in some wonder. "On the contrary, every sentinel who came upon post

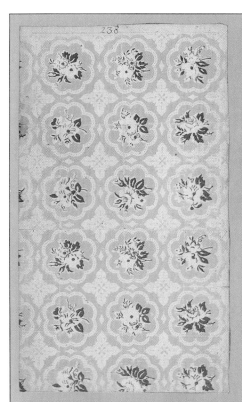

An excerpt (*right*) from the Vicksburg *Daily Citizen* of July 4, 1863, consists of a challenge to Grant and a jubilant Federal rejoinder. The edition had been set in type on July 2, but was abandoned when the city surrendered. The Federal occupiers then printed the issue — on the back side of wallpaper (*above*) because of a newsprint shortage — after adding their gleeful "Note" boasting about the victory.

ON DIT.—That the great Ulysses—the Yankee Generalissimo, surnamed Grant—has expressed his intention of dining in Vicksburg on Saturday next, and celebrating the 4th of July by a grand dinner, and so forth. When asked if he would invite Gen. Jo. Johnston to join, he said: "No! for fear there will be a row at the table." Ulysses must get into the city before he dines in it. The way to cook a rabbit is "first catch the rabbit," &c.

NOTE.

JULY 4th, 1863.

Two days bring about great changes. The banner of the Union floats over Vicksburg. Gen. Grant has "caught the rabbit;" he has dined in Vicksburg, and he did bring his dinner with him. The "Citizen" lives to see it. For the last time it appears on "Wall-paper." No more will it eulogize the luxury of mule meat and fricassed kitten—urge Southern warriors to such diet nevermore. This is the last wall paper edition, and is, excepting this note, from the types as we found them. It will be valuable hereafter as a curiosity.

brought haversacks filled with provisions, which he would give to some famished Southerner with the remark, 'Here, Reb, I know you are starved nearly to death.' "

Colonel Samuel Lockett, Pemberton's chief engineer, later remembered that the only Federal cheers he heard that day came from a Union outfit that raised a shout "for the gallant defenders of Vicksburg."

The fall of Vicksburg was greeted with shock and grief in the South. As many there soon recognized, July 4, 1863, marked the turning point of the Civil War, for on that same day, in the East, Robert E. Lee had retreated after three days of battle at Gettysburg. General Josiah Gorgas, the Confederacy's chief of ordnance, wrote in his diary: "It seems incredible that human power could effect such a change in so brief a space. Yesterday we rode on the pinnacle of success — today absolute ruin seems our portion. The Confederacy totters to its destruction."

In the North, people were still observing the victory at Gettysburg when word came of the Vicksburg triumph, and the celebrations surged anew. "The whole country is joyous," wrote Secretary of the Navy Gideon Welles. There were 100-gun salutes in half a dozen cities, and churches observed the occasion with the tolling of bells.

President Lincoln was both relieved and gratified by the news. A few days later he sent an extraordinary letter to Ulysses S. Grant. "My Dear General," the President began. "I do not remember that you and I ever met personally. I write this now as a grateful acknowledgement for the almost inestimable service you have done the country. I wish to say a word further. When you first reached the vicinity of Vicksburg, I

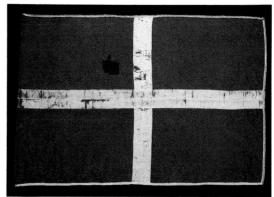

thought you should do what you finally did — march the troops across the neck, run the batteries with the transports, and thus go below; and I never had any faith, except a general hope that you knew better than I, that the Yazoo Pass expedition and the like could succeed. When you got below and took Port Gibson, Grand Gulf and vicinity, I thought you should go down the river and join General Banks; and when you turned northward, east of the Big Black, I feared it was a mistake. I now wish to make a personal acknowledgement that you were right and I was wrong."

On July 9, the Confederate commander at Port Hudson, having learned of Vicksburg's fall, surrendered the garrison. The Mississippi River was at last open to Union shipping along its entire length. On July 16, the unarmed cargo steamer *Imperial* arrived at New Orleans flying the Stars and Stripes, having left St. Louis eight days earlier.

The following month, Abraham Lincoln, speaking on the progress of the War, summed up the year's achievement along the Mississippi in a few felicitous words that rang with triumph and satisfaction. "The Father of Waters," he said, "again goes unvexed to the sea."

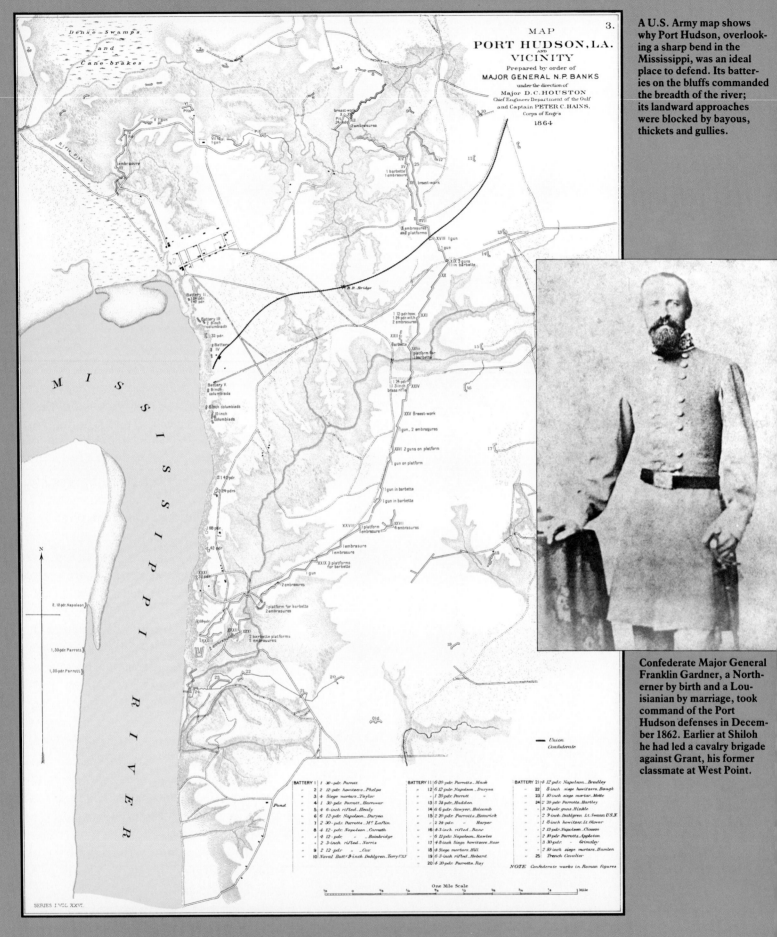

MAP
PORT HUDSON, LA.
AND
VICINITY
Prepared by order of
MAJOR GENERAL N.P. BANKS
under the direction of
Major D.C. HOUSTON
Chief Engineer Department of the Gulf
and Captain PETER C. HAINS.
Corps of Eng'rs
1864

3.

A U.S. Army map shows why Port Hudson, overlooking a sharp bend in the Mississippi, was an ideal place to defend. Its batteries on the bluffs commanded the breadth of the river; its landward approaches were blocked by bayous, thickets and gullies.

Confederate Major General Franklin Gardner, a Northerner by birth and a Louisianian by marriage, took command of the Port Hudson defenses in December 1862. Earlier at Shiloh he had led a cavalry brigade against Grant, his former classmate at West Point.

160

SERIES I VOL XXVI.

One Mile Scale

— Union
  Confederate

NOTE Confederate works in Roman figures

Port Hudson: The Final Fortress

Vicksburg was not the only Confederate obstacle blocking the Mississippi early in 1863. On a bluff 300 river miles downstream sat Port Hudson, Louisiana, a town hemmed in on the landward side by woods, swamps and ravines. In the words of a private garrisoned there, it was "a place hard to get at." It was also a place of great strategic importance. Not only did Port Hudson menace Federal ships heading north against Vicksburg, it also guarded the nearby Red River, down which flowed goods from the West that sustained the Confederacy.

The Confederates had fortified Port Hudson by mounting 19 guns along the bluff and by erecting earthworks around the landward side. The residents had departed, to be replaced by 16,000 troops under Major General Franklin Gardner.

As spring approached, Port Hudson was a source of frustration for the Union's Nathaniel P. Banks, commander of the Department of the Gulf. Banks had orders to open the Mississippi and he was eager to comply, hoping to restore a military reputation badly tarnished back east in the Shenandoah Valley and at Cedar Mountain. In April he would launch an effort to secure territory west of Port Hudson. But Banks lacked the manpower to attack or besiege the port itself; the best he could do that March was agree to feign an attack while part of Admiral Farragut's fleet ran past the river batteries to isolate Port Hudson from the north. So began a four-month-long campaign that taxed the will of both sides — and exacted a high price in blood.

One of the gun emplacements that made Port Hudson unassailable from the Mississippi River sits atop a craggy 80-foot bluff in a view looking downstream.

Admiral Farragut's Fiery Passage

In early March, Banks began his feint on Port Hudson from the south with 12,000 men, and Farragut designated seven vessels, led by his flagship, the *Hartford*, to run the gantlet. The ironclad *Essex* and six mortar schooners were to stay back and lend support. "The best protection against the enemy's fire," Farragut told his sailors, "is a well-directed fire from our own guns."

By March 14, the warships were in position below Port Hudson and the army was poised within six miles of town. Banks and Farragut agreed to make their move that night. But the troops got bogged down and arrived at Port Hudson too late to create a diversion. In the words of one disgruntled officer, Banks's men turned out to be "little more than spectators of the battle." And a stirring sight it was. "Heavy shells were falling fast and thick," a Confederate later wrote. "It seemed as if the whole heavens were ablaze with thunder and lightning."

Fires lit on the western bank outlined the fleet as it headed upriver, hugging the eastern shore to avoid shoals. Farragut's three gunboats were lashed to the sides of his larger sloops for protection, and the side-wheeler *Mississippi* brought up the rear.

The Federal vessels came under fire, and before long four of them were sorely damaged and had to turn back. A fifth vessel, the *Mississippi*, ran aground and was blown up by her crew. The *Hartford*, with the *Albatross* lashed to her side, also ran aground, but after several awful minutes the flagship pulled free, aided by the smaller vessel, and both struggled upstream past the forts.

The casualties were one-sided. The Federals lost 121 men, including 84 dead. The Confederates suffered only one dead and 19 wounded. But now Farragut had Port Hudson bracketed by Federal warships.

Confederate guns high above the Mississippi at Port Hudson pummel Farragut's fleet. At far left, the side-wheeler *Mississippi* is afire.

Squeezing the Vise

MAJOR GENERAL NATHANIEL P. BANKS

By early May, the Port Hudson garrison had been reduced to less than 6,000 men, as about half of Gardner's troops had been sent north to reinforce John Pemberton. Banks (*left*), who had been clearing out pockets of resistance on the western side of the Mississippi, saw his chance. He ordered 24,000 men to cross the river north of the stronghold. At about the same time a division of 6,000 men, along with two regiments of Louisiana blacks, moved up from the south.

On May 19, General Joseph E. Johnston, overall Confederate commander in the West, ordered Gardner to evacuate and retreat to Jackson. But by the time the order arrived, the Federals already had Port Hudson in a vise.

Beneath live oaks draped in Spanish moss, a Federal baggage train, escorted by infantry and mounted officers, crosses Bayou Montecino on the road north to Port Hudson.

The 1st Indiana Heavy Artillery forms at Baton Rouge before advancing north against Port Hudson. The Battery's 20-pounder Parrott rifles were so heavy that they were pulled by mules rather than horses.

A Grueling Standoff in the Louisiana Sun

"Beware Yankees!" warned a crude sign carved into a tree trunk outside Port Hudson. "This road leads to hell." Indeed, the six-week siege that began in the suffocating heat of late May became a hellish nightmare for both sides.

With a force several times the size of the Confederate garrison, Banks might have let time do his work. But he was impatient. On May 27, he launched an all-out attack through the tangled underbrush and fallen timbers bordering the Confederate earthworks. The effort failed, and his men were driven back with heavy losses. "It was difficult not only to move but even to see," fumed one Federal officer. "The affair was a gigantic bushwhack."

On June 14, the Federals attacked once more, and again the result was a bloody repulse. The failed attacks had cost the Federals nearly 4,000 dead and wounded. Another 7,000 men had fallen ill, many with dysentery and sunstroke.

But the Confederates were also hurting. Although they had suffered fewer than 700 casualties, sickness spread as supplies ran low and the men were reduced to drinking stagnant water and eating mules and rats.

Federal infantrymen clamber over fallen timbers in an attack on Port Hudson. Thrown back at great loss, the Federals cursed the thicket in front of the Confederate works. One soldier called it "the bloody chasm."

Outside Port Hudson, Confederate defenders have cut down magnolia trees and amassed underbrush to clear a field of fire and block the enemy's path. The cavalier of stacked hogsheads at rear was built up by the Federals from within their trenchworks to provide a platform for observers and sharpshooters.

An End to the Ordeal

In early July, Federal sappers dug tunnels to within yards of the Confederate works. Banks planned to blast holes in the defenses with heavy mines and send in a storming party of 1,000 volunteers. Most of the Federals thought it a foolhardy idea.

Two days before the scheduled attack, word arrived that Vicksburg had fallen. Port Hudson was now truly isolated. Further fighting seemed senseless, and a truce was called. Men of both sides crawled from their trenches to shake hands. On July 9, the surrender was official. The Confederacy's final fortress on the Mississippi was no more.

The muzzle of this 24-pounder rifle at Port Hudson was blown away by a Federal shell.

These dugouts, burrowed in the earth at Port Hudson's strongest redoubt, the Citadel, protected their occupants from all but a direct hit.

After the siege, the section of the defense line called "Fort Desperate" by the Confederates is a shambles of timbers and wrecked cannon.

BIBLIOGRAPHY

Books

Badeau, Adam, *Military History of Ulysses S. Grant, from April, 1861, to April, 1865.* D. Appleton and Company, 1885.

Bearss, Edwin C.:
Rebel Victory at Vicksburg. Vicksburg Centennial Commemoration Commission, 1963.
The Siege of Jackson, July 10-17, 1863. Gateway Press, Inc., 1981.
Three Other Post-Vicksburg Actions. Gateway Press, Inc., 1981.

Bearss, Edwin C., and Warren Grabau, *The Battle of Jackson, May 14, 1863.* Gateway Press, Inc., 1981.

Bennett, L. G., and Wm. M. Haigh, *History of the Thirty-sixth Regiment Illinois Volunteers, during the War of the Rebellion.* Knickerbocker & Hodder, 1876.

Beyer, W. F., and O. F. Keydel, eds., *Deeds of Valor from Records in the Archives of the United States Government: How American Heroes Won the Medal of Honor.* The Perrien-Keydel Company, 1906.

Boatner, Mark Mayo, III, *The Civil War Dictionary.* David McKay Company, Inc., 1959.

Brown, D. Alexander, *Grierson's Raid.* Press of Morningside Bookshop, 1981.

Cadwallader, Sylvanus, *Three Years with Grant as Recalled by a War Correspondent.* Ed. by Benjamin P. Thomas. Alfred A. Knopf, 1955.

Carleton, Mark T., *River Capital: An Illustrated History of Baton Rouge.* Windsor Publications, Inc., 1981.

Carter, Samuel, III, *The Final Fortress: The Campaign for Vicksburg, 1862-1863.* St. Martin's Press, 1980.

Catton, Bruce:
Grant Moves South. Little, Brown and Company, 1960.
Grant Takes Command. Little, Brown and Company, 1969.

Committee of the Regiment, *Military History and Reminiscences of the Thirteenth Regiment of Illinois Volunteer Infantry in the Civil War in the United States, 1861-1865.* Women's Temperance Publishing Association, 1892.

Congdon, Don, ed., *Combat: The Civil War.* Delacorte Press, 1967.

Cotton, Gordon A.:
The Old Court House. Keith Printing Company, Inc., 1982.
Yankee Bullets, Rebel Rations. Keith Printing Company, Inc., 1984.

Crandall, Warren Daniel, *History of the Ram Fleet and Mississippi Marine Brigade in the War for the Union on the Mississippi and Its Tributaries: The Story of the Ellets and Their Men.* Buschart Brothers, 1907.

Crooke, George, *The Twenty-first Regiment of Iowa Volunteer Infantry: A Narrative of Its Experience in Active Service.* King, Fowle & Co., 1891.

Cunningham, Edward, *The Port Hudson Campaign, 1862-1863.* Louisiana State University Press, 1963.

Currie, George E., *Warfare along the Mississippi: The Letters of Lieutenant Colonel George E. Currie.* Ed. by Norman E. Clarke Sr. Clarke Historical Collection, 1961.

Dana, Charles A., *Recollections of the Civil War: With the Leaders at Washington and in the Field in the Sixties.* D. Appleton and Company, 1902.

Davis, William C., ed., *Fighting for Time (The Image of War, 1861-1865, Vol. 4).* Doubleday & Company, Inc., 1983.

De Forest, John William, *A Volunteer's Adventures: A Union Captain's Record of the Civil War.* Ed. by James H. Croushore. Yale University Press, 1946.

Edmonds, David C., *The Guns of Port Hudson,* Vol. 1. The Acadiana Press, 1983.

Foote, Shelby, *The Civil War: A Narrative,* 3 vols. Random House, 1958, 1963 and 1974.

Fox, William F., *Regimental Losses in the American Civil War, 1861-1865.* Albany Publishing Company, 1889.

Frost, M. O., *Regimental History of the Tenth Missouri Volunteer Infantry.* M. O. Frost Printing Company, 1892.

Grant, Jesse R., *In the Days of My Father General Grant.* Harper & Brothers Publishers, 1925.

Grant, U. S., *Personal Memoirs of U. S. Grant.* Charles L. Webster & Company, 1894.

Groce, George C., and David H. Wallace, *The New-York Historical Society's Dictionary of Artists in America, 1564-1860.* Yale University Press, 1957.

Hartpence, Wm. R., *History of the Fifty-first Indiana Veteran Volunteer Infantry from 1861 to 1866.* The Robert Clarke Company, 1894.

Heitman, Francis B., *Historical Register and Dictionary of the United States Army, from Its Organization, September 29, 1789, to March 2, 1903.* University of Illinois Press, 1965.

Henry, Robert Selph, *"First with the Most" Forrest.* The Bobbs-Merrill Company, 1944.

Hoehling, A. A., *Vicksburg: 47 Days of Siege.* Prentice-Hall, Inc., 1969.

Howell, H. Grady, Jr., *Going to Meet the Yankees: A History of the "Bloody Sixth" Mississippi Infantry, C.S.A.* Chickasaw Bayou Press, 1981.

Hutchins, Edward Ridgeway, *The War of the Sixties.* The Neale Publishing Company, 1912.

Johnson, James Ralph, Alfred Hoyt Bill and Hirst Dillon Milhollen, *Horsemen Blue and Gray: A Pictorial History.* Oxford University Press, 1960.

Johnson, Robert Underwood, and Clarence Clough Buel, eds., *Battles and Leaders of the Civil War,* Vol. 3. The Century Co., 1884.

Jones, S. C., *Reminiscences of the Twenty-second Iowa Volunteer Infantry.* Iowa City, 1907.

Korn, Bertram W., *American Jewry and the Civil War.* Cleveland World Publishing Company, 1961.

Lewis, Gene D., *Charles Ellett, Jr.: The Engineer as Individualist.* University of Illinois Press, 1968.

Lewis, Henry, *The Valley of the Mississippi Illustrated.* Ed. by Bertha L. Heilbron, transl. by A. Hermina Poatgieter. Minnesota Historical Society, 1967.

Lewis, Lloyd:
Captain Sam Grant. Little, Brown and Company, 1950.
Sherman: Fighting Prophet. Harcourt, Brace and Company, 1932.

Loughborough, Mary Ann (Webster), *My Cave Life in Vicksburg.* D. Appleton and Company, 1864.

McFeely, William S., *Grant: A Biography.* W. W. Norton & Company, 1981.

Miers, Earl Schenck, *The Web of Victory: Grant at Vicksburg.* Alfred A. Knopf, 1955.

Miller, Francis Trevelyan, ed., *The Photographic History of the Civil War,* Vols. 1, 2 and 6. The Review of Reviews Co., 1912.

Oldroyd, Osborn H., *A Soldier's Story of the Siege of Vicksburg, from the Diary of Osborn H. Oldroyd.* H. W. Rokker, Printer, 1885.

Porter, David D., *The Naval History of the Civil War.* The Sherman Publishing Company, 1886.

Pryor, Sara Agnes (Rice), *Reminiscences of Peace and War.* The Macmillan Company, 1904.

Raphael, Morris, *The Battle in the Bayou Country.* Harlo Press, 1975.

Reed, Rowena, *Combined Operations in the Civil War.* Naval Institute Press, 1978.

Russell, William Howard, *My Diary North and South.* Peter Smith, 1954.

Samuels, Peggy and Harold, *The Illustrated Biographical Encyclopedia of Artists of the American West.* Doubleday & Company, Inc., 1976.

Sandburg, Carl, *Abraham Lincoln: The War Years,* 4 vols. Harcourt, Brace & World, Inc., 1939.

Sherman, William T.:
Home Letters of General Sherman. Ed. by Mark Anthony De Wolfe Howe. Charles Scribner's Sons, 1909.
Memoirs of General William T. Sherman. Indiana University Press, 1957.

Smith, John Thomas, *A History of the Thirty-first Regiment of Indiana Volunteer Infantry in the War of the Rebellion.* Western Methodist Book Concern, 1900.

Starr, Louis, *Bohemian Brigade: Civil War Newsmen in Action.* Alfred A. Knopf, 1954.

Todd, Frederick P., *American Military Equipage, 1851-1872.* Charles Scribner's Sons, 1974.

Trimble, Harvey M., ed., *History of the Ninety-third Regiment Illinois Volunteer Infantry from Organization to Muster Out.* The Blakely Printing Co., 1898.

United States Navy Department:
Civil War Naval Chronology, 1861-1865. U.S. Government Printing Office, 1971.
Official Records of the Union and Confederate Navies in the War of the Rebellion. U.S. Government Printing Office, 1912.

United States War Department, *The War of the Rebellion: A Compilation of the Official Records of the Union and Confederate Armies,* U.S. Government Printing Office, 1902.

Walker, Peter F., *Vicksburg: A People at War, 1860-1865.* The University of North Carolina Press, 1960.

Warner, Ezra J.:
Generals in Blue. Louisiana State University Press, 1964.
Generals in Gray. Louisiana State University Press, 1959.

Webb, Willard, ed., *Crucial Moments of the Civil War.* Fountainhead Publishers, Inc., 1961.

Weisberger, Bernard A., *Reporters for the Union.* Little, Brown and Company, 1953.

West, Richard S., Jr.:
Mr. Lincoln's Navy. Longmans, Green and Company, 1957.
The Second Admiral: A Life of David Dixon Porter, 1813-1891. Coward-McCann, Inc., 1937.

Wheeler, Richard, *We Knew William Tecumseh Sherman.* Thomas Y. Crowell Company, 1977.

Williams, George Washington, *A History of the Negro Troops in the War of the Rebellion, 1861-65.* Bergman Publishers, 1968.

Williams, Kenneth P., *Lincoln Finds a General: A Military Study of the Civil War,* Vol. 3. The Macmillan Company, 1952.

Willis, Henry Augustus, *The Fifty-third Regiment Massachusetts Volunteers, Comprising Also a History of the Siege of Port Hudson.* Press of Blanchard & Brown, 1889.

Wilson, James Harrison, *Under the Old Flag: Recollections of Military Operations in the War for the Union, the Spanish War, the Boxer Rebellion, etc.* Greenwood Press, 1971.

Winters, John D., *The Civil War in Louisiana.* Louisiana State University Press, 1963.

Other Sources

Abbott, John S. C., "Heroic Deeds of Heroic Men." *Harper's New Monthly Magazine*, February 1865.

Ballard, Michael B., "The Battle of Baton Rouge." *Civil War Times Illustrated*, February 1981.

"Bombardment of Grand Gulf." *Frank Leslie's Illustrated Newspaper*, May 30, 1863.

Castel, Albert, "Victory at Corinth." *Civil War Times Illustrated*, October 1978.

"Chickasaw Bluffs: Sherman's Attack on the Rear of Vicksburg." *National Tribune*, August 7, 1884.

"Col. Grierson." *Frank Leslie's Illustrated Newspaper*, June 6, 1863.

Dickinson, John N., "The Civil War Years of John Alexander Logan." *Journal of the Illinois State Historical Society*, summer 1963.

Dihel, R. M., "Champion's Hill." *National Tribune*, September 11, 1884.

Harris, J. B., "An Incident of Champion's Hill: General Logan's Advance." *National Tribune*, July 31, 1884.

Huffstot, Robert S., "Battle for Post of Arkansas." *Civil War Times Illustrated*, January 1969.

Labuzan, Charles A., "Corinth: A Rebel Officer's Account of His Experience in That Fight." *National Tribune*, December 4, 1884.

Lord, Francis A., "The Ketchum Hand Grenade." *Civil War Times Illustrated*, June 1967.

Morris, D. C., "Vicksburg: A Graphic Description of the Charge." *National Tribune*, October 23, 1884.

Ridley, S. J., "Concerning the Siege at Vicksburg." *Confederate Veteran*, Vol. 2, 1894.

"Struggle for Vicksburg." *Civil War Times Illustrated*, July 1967.

PICTURE CREDITS

ACKNOWLEDGMENTS

The editors thank the following individuals and institutions for their help in the preparation of this volume:

Illinois: Peoria — Sherri Schneider, Special Collections Center, Cullom-Davis Library, Bradley University. Springfield — Mary Michals, Illinois State Historical Library.

Louisiana: Baton Rouge — Charles East. Lafayette — David C. Edmonds, University of Southwestern Louisiana. New Orleans — Richard C. Marvin, The Historic New Orleans Collection.

Mississippi: Corinth — Margaret Greene Rogers. Jackson — Marian Bourdeaux, Public Information Office, State of Mississippi Department of Archives and History. Port Gibson — Helen Slay, Grand Gulf Military State Park. Vicksburg — Gordon A. Cotton, Old Court House Museum; C. Bowie Lanford, Vicksburg National Military Park.

Pennsylvania: Philadelphia — Mr. and Mrs. Manuel Kean, Kean Archives.

Texas: Austin — Lawrence T. Jones, Confederate Calendar Works.

Virginia: Quantico — Anthony Tommell, The Marine Corps Museum.

Washington, D.C.: Harry Hunter, National Museum of American History, Smithsonian Institution; Oscar Fitzgerald, U.S. Navy Memorial Museum.

The index for this book was prepared by Nicholas J. Anthony.

INDEX